**EDUCATION
TRAINING
YOUTH**

**Study group on
education and training**

# Report

# Accomplishing Europe through education and training

**EUROPEAN
COMMISSION**

A great deal of additional information on the European Union is available on the Internet.
It can be accessed through the Europa server (http://europa.eu.int)

Cataloguing data can be found at the end of this publication

Luxembourg: Office for Official Publications of the European Communities, 1997

ISBN 92-827-9493-8

*Printed in Italy*

# Groupe de réflexion sur l'éducation et la formation

Jean Louis REIFFERS
Président du Groupe de réflexion sur l'éducation et la formation

à

Madame Edith CRESSON
Membre de la Commission,

Madame la Commissaire,

J'ai l'honneur de vous transmettre ce rapport sur l'éducation et la formation en Europe au nom des membres du Groupe de réflexion sur l'éducation et la formation que vous avez mis en place le 21 septembre 1995.

Grâce à la bienveillance de la Direction générale XXII — Education, Formation, Jeunesse — et à l'aide constante du Secrétariat qu'elle a mis à notre disposition, nous avons pu développer nos idées et mener nos débats dans la plus grande indépendance. Chaque membre du Groupe a eu à coeur de respecter la règle du jeu que nous nous sommes fixée, a savoir, développer ses appréciations à partir de ses opinions personnelles, indépendamment de toute appartenance nationale, professionnelle ou culturelle.

Cette règle du jeu nous a permis d'envisager plusieurs facettes de l'éducation et de la formation et nous a conduit à une conclusion qui oriente tout ce rapport: l'Union européenne doit proposer, en étroite relation avec les Etats membres, un «rêve européen» à sa jeunesse et s'appuyer sur l'éducation et la formation pour ce faire.

Les membres du groupe de réflexion vous remercient, par mon intermédiaire, de la confiance que vous leur avez accordée.

Jean-Louis REIFFERS

# Table of contents

# Report of the study group on education and training

## Foreword

Education and training stand at the centre of debate on the future of our societies and European integration. For the future of European integration itself, and at a time during which the IGC will be taking its decisions on the directions in which to move, bringing Europe and its citizens closer together has been viewed as a central axis. The many events and activities carried out in 1996 within the framework of the European year of Lifelong Learning have shown that access to the educational dimension for all constitutes an essential lever to build a People's Europe.

Mindful of these issues, the Commission has launched an in-depth discussion on the guidelines for action proposed by its White Paper 'Teaching and Learning: towards the learning society' which was adopted in November 1996.

To study the axes opened up in the White Paper in greater detail, and to pursue a number of education and training policy issues related to these axes, the Commission established a Study Group on Education and Training in July 1995. Twenty-five high-level experts were nominated by the Commission on the basis of their expertise and reputation in the academic world and in the worlds of policy and practice. Those experts selected represent a variety of concerned constituencies: companies, trades unions, schools, vocational training bodies, adult education and universities.

By definition, the Study Group is made up of independent experts, whereby the Commission's intention was to ensure the representation of all fifteen Member States. At the same time of course, the views expressed by the members of the Group have not been made on behalf of an individual Member State, in that the experts concerned were nominated by the Commission and not by the Member States themselves.

The established mandate of the Study Group was a very broad-ranging one. Its work was directed towards a primarily prospective purpose, with the aim of generating a fully open debate on future developments. Therefore, the Study Group's terms of reference specified that the themes to be discussed could be selected on its own initiative, but also at the request of the Commission. This led to the identification of two operational working levels for the Group's work. On the one hand, it has worked reactively, primarily by contributing its views to the White Paper *Teaching and Learning* and to the launch of the European Year of Lifelong Learning. On the other hand, the Study Group has established and developed its own ideas on the basis of themes determined on its own initiative.

This report is the outcome of the Study Group's ideas and contributions in this latter, proactive, mode. The members of the Group have therefore contributed, in their various ways, to the report on the basis of jointly-defined themes and an agreed plan. This report thus results from a group of independent experts brought together by the Commission. It is not an official Commission document. The Commission, for its part, facilitated the organisation of the Study Group's work and provided a secretariat to support the work of its members and chairperson in their reflections and in the production of the report. DG XXII representatives, and in particular the Director-General and Directors, also intervened in and contributed to the debates.

The Commission has wished to encourage a wide-ranging and open debate and within this perspective supports the publication and broad dissemination of the report, which synthesises the Study Group's debates. It considers the report to be a major contribution of high intellectual ambition, which will enrich further reflection as the part of all those concerned with education and training.

# The study group members

**Chairperson**
Prof. Jean-Louis REIFFERS
Professeur, doyen honoraire de la Faculté des Sciences économiques de l'Université de la Méditerranée
Chairperson of the Study Group

**Committee members**
Prof. Roberto CARNEIRO
Universidade Católica Portuguesa

Prof. Ginevra CONTI-ODORISIO
Università di Roma 3 (Histoire des doctrines politiques)
Università LUISS (Histoire de la question féminine)

Prof. John COOLAHAN
Saint Patrick's College
University of Maynooth

Dr. David MARSDEN
Reader in Industrial Relations
London School of Economics

Prof. Martin TWARDY
Wirtschafts- und Sozialwissenschaftliche Fakultät der Universität zu Köln

**Members**
Prof. Giuseppe AIROLDI
Prorettore, Università «L. Bocconi»

Prof. Drª Maria Teresa AMBROSIO
Professeur de l'Universidade Nova de Lisboa

M. Wenceslas BAUDRILLART
Ancien Conseiller social du Premier Ministre
Responsable des Ressources humaines

Chairman Dr. Erhard BUSEK
Former Vice-Chancellor and Federal Minister
Institute for the Danube Region and Central Europe

Prof. Oriol HOMS
Sociologue
Directeur de la Fondation CIREM

Dr. Ian JOHNSTON CB
Deputy Principal, Sheffield Hallam University

Ms. Helene LUND
Deputy Mayor
Vice-Chair of Commission 6 (Committee of the Regions)

Prof. Beatriz MUÑOZ-SECA
Instituto de Estudios Superiores de la Empresa, Universidad de Navarra

Prof. Britta NAUMANN
GEW-Hauptvorstand

Prof. Nicos D. POLYDORIDES
University of Patras - URSA-NET

Prof. Paul QUINTAS
The Open University School of Management

Prof. Aino SALLINEN
Rector of the University of Jyväskylä

Dr. Walter SCHUSSER
Vice-President, SIEMENS AG

M. Claude THELOT
Directeur de l'Evaluation et de la Prospective
Ministère de l'Education nationale, de l'Enseignement supérieur, et de la
Recherche

M. Henri THYES
Membre du Comité de Direction à la Banque du Luxembourg s.a.


Ms. Kerstin THOURSIE
Assistant Under-Secretary
Swedish Ministry of Education and Science

The Group's views have been synthesised from the views expressed by its individual members. The report therefore reflects a majority consensus within the Group, but not necessarily unanimity on all matters. With regard to Chapter VI on education and training systems and their actors, the Group would have liked to have taken its analysis further. It was unable to do so in the time available during the past year and deems it necessary to extend debate and analysis in this field, in particular using the descriptive statistical data attached to this report as a starting-point.

# Study group on education and training report 'accomplishing europe through education and training'

## Executive summary

If Europe is to remain at the driving edge, economic and political progress must be complemented by offering an 'European vision' to her young people. Education and training efforts must mobilize themselves around this emerging picture.

This task is an urgent one: whilst the European population is stabilizing, and the proportion of young Europeans within the total is continually diminishing, the world's population will almost double in the space of the next generation. Mobilizing education and training effort is also urgent in the interests of those adults with low levels of education and qualifications, and those who must renew their personal competencies on a lifelong basis. Finally, this task is an urgent one in order to facilitate the best adaptation possible to new employment conditions and the development of the learning society.

Positions within the world system are now being defined. These changes correspond to a sentiment of uncertainty, which at times can lead us to think that human understanding of the world is on the retreat. Nevertheless, the Study Group takes the view that technology and international competition present opportunities that can be grasped.

Their different origins notwithstanding, the Study Group members are in agreement that Europe's education and training systems must take three major imperatives into account: (i) the need to strengthen European competitiveness in economic, technological, innovatory scientific and organizational terms; (ii) the need to appreciate the difficulties of the current situation; (iii) the need to respect the basic principles of education, whose aims go far beyond a purely utilitarian perspective.

During the course of a heritage accumulated over the centuries, three fundamental aims of education and training have emerged through a long process of maturation. These are, firstly, the development of personal autonomy; secondly, the stimulation of opportunities for social integration and, thirdly, the improvement of vocational competencies. In consolidating these three fundamental aims and in building upon this heritage, educational and training systems can better respond to the imperatives noted above.

In order to propose a European vision to its young people, Europe must take a step forward in the field of education and training. Whilst many routes are possible in lending content to this vision, the aims to be attained should be commonly shared. The Study Group considers that changes required in education and training systems should envisage four aims, significant progress towards which should be made between now and the year 2000. These aims are: (i) constructing European citizenship through education and training; (ii) reinforcing European competitiveness and preserving employment through education and training; (iii) maintaining social cohesion through education and training; (iv) education and training in the information society. In order to address more specifically the question of implementing these changes, the Study Group turned its attention to the conditions under which education and training systems function and to the actors who are entrusted with this task, in particular schoolteachers and heads of education establishments.

## 'Constructing European citizenship through education and training'

European citizenship is above all a humanist concept, founded in the construction of a greater Europe characterized by cultural differences, by different economic conceptions, and by different natural realities — but united by the sense of belonging to a common civilization. It is on the basis of a shared democratic culture that this greater Europe will construct itself and in which Europeans will recognize themselves as citizens of Europe. They will not regard themselves as citizens of Europe because they belong to a common culture, or on the basis of a particular dimension of belonging. Rather, they will do so because they will construct themselves as citizens of Europe on the basis of new relations which they will establish between themselves. This is the first element of a European vision to propose to young people.

To become a rallying idea, European citizenship must be real, not merely formal. This implies going beyond principles and rules. Citizenship is a plural concept: (i) it is a normative idea and in this sense is related to the concept of civil society and its moral and ideological defence; (ii) it is a social practice and develops through dynamic process, during which the sense of belonging constructs itself on the basis of differences, of communication with others, of conflicts and negotiated compromises, and of shared images; (iii) it is a relational practice between individuals in their social context at the level of state, local government, and associations.

The education system has a role to play in the promotion of active citizenship. Education can play this role through its formal institutions, but it can also do so through communities or through the mass-media. Under varying names, education for citizenship exists in many Member States. It pursues different aims, takes up varying amounts of curriculum time and addresses itself to different age groups and target groups. If we wish to develop a sense of being citizens of Europe amongst young people, some improvement in this field is therefore necessary.

From this point of view and in considering the path to be followed, the question of gender relations is significant, but equally that of intercultural relations. The history of the long struggle for women's rights is a good example of the effort that is needed in order to learn to relativize seemingly universal values, but without falling into a moral vacuum. It also shows that formal rights, however dearly bought, can be contradicted in practice: numerous forms of implicit discrimination still exist, which are based on apparently flattering differentiation, but which in fact lead to constraints for those individuals at hand, limiting them to circumscribed and highly specified responsibilities. To counter these practices, Europe must promote education and training that aims to destroy all stereotypical images of human beings.

For the purposes of developing a programme of citizenship education the following five essential dimensions have been retained in this report. These are: (i) the recognition of the dignity and centrality of the human person; (ii) social citizenship, social rights and responsibilities, the struggle against social exclusion; (iii) egalitarian citizenship, that is, the rejection of discrimination and prejudice based on gender and ethnicity; understanding the value of equality; (iv) intercultural citizenship: the value of diversity and openness for a plural world; (v) ecological citizenship.

In close liaison with Member States, **Europe should take action** through education and training to consolidate European citizenship in the three following domains: (i) to affirm and transmit the common values on which its civilization is founded; (ii) to assist in devising and disseminating ways of enabling young people to play a fuller part as European citizens, with a particular focus on teaching and learning; (iii) to identify and disseminate the best practice in education and training for citizenship in order to filter out the best means of acquiring the elements of European citizenship, and by initiating experimental projects which permit concrete forms of implementation.

**The common values** of European civilization upon which the Study Group have agreed are the following:

- human rights/human dignity

- fundamental freedoms

- democratic legitimacy

- peace and the rejection of violence as a means to an end

- respect for others

- a spirit of solidarity (within Europe and vis-à-vis the world as a whole)

- equitable development

- equal opportunities

- the principles of rational thought: the ethics of evidence and proof

- preservation of the ecosystem

- personal responsibility

New forms of co-operation must be developed for teaching these values. Increasing teaching contact hours to make space for civic education as a distinct subject, substituting civic education for other curriculum subjects, or developing a corps of specialised civics teachers are not the routes to follow. Civics education is a task for all schoolteachers, and thus we might rather envisage:

- studying in detail the key issues of discrimination among citizens, particularly those relating to the issue of gender and inter-ethnic relations;

- promoting university research on these issues;

- highlighting European achievements in the arts and sciences as a common heritage for all citizens;

- in the teaching of history, social science or literature, presenting analyses for those social, political and ethnic conflicts which lead to violence in Europe itself and in Europe's bordering regions.

As far as methods are concerned, a citizenship pedagogy must be developed. There is a need to encourage all active pedagogies, which are based on fostering critical awareness and independence of reasoning and groupwork. The development of the most significant current advance in this field, border pedagogy, is included in this category. Border pedagogy is a strategy for learning about the cultural Other, by looking critically at how images, representations and texts are constructed and at their hidden messages. This approach facilitates learning how to identify one's own 'borders', those of others, and the borders of the external social world. Learning to appreciate differences as a positive opportunity must become one of the key competencies for Europeans. To this end, it would be desirable:

- to improve both knowledge of foreign languages and understanding of European cultures;

- to modernise history and geography curricula, which implies, in particular, a process of 'disarmament' of educational content — which is often inspired by nationally based views of wars and conflicts;

- to support democratic styles of governance of educational establishments;

- to invest in the training of teachers and heads of establishment and to facilitate their mobility within Europe.

In considering those experiences that deserve impulse and dissemination at European level, the intercultural school is an apposite example. In liaison with the Member States, Europe must equip itself with the means for developing exemplary experiences of interculturality in the school. The intercultural school already empirically exists in the prestigious international schools and in those schools in areas with a high concentration of immigrants. The intercultural school must nevertheless be thought through on a broader scale, because interculturality in the school focuses the whole problematic of citizenship. This kind of school must become an experimental field with a view to preparing for its implementation on a wider front, in that multiculturality is an inevitability simply as a consequence of demographic trends.

## 'Reinforcing European competitiveness and preserving employment through education and training'

The threats posed for European competitiveness are currently underestimated. Education and training systems are insufficiently aware of the constraints of competitivity. Education and training systems cannot be held responsible for rising unemployment, but they nevertheless carry essential responsibility for knowledge transmission and for equipping young Europeans with the appropriate skills, qualifications and attitudes essential to confronting this challenge well.

The principal long term and valid option for promoting European competitivity in the market is to ensure a strong capacity in the quest for quality and innovation. In adapting to the characteristics of future-oriented enterprise, education and training systems could contribute to European competitivity and to the maintenance of employment. Through innovation and personal initiative, Europe could develop productive service sector employment and self-employment.

**Placing quality at the centre** implies taking into account, as optimally as possible, those for whom the service is provided: this goal must be returned to the foreground of concern. From this point of view, the direction to be taken by our systems of education and training is clear: they must orient themselves to those occupations most in demand. This means: being fully cognisant with the nature of this demand; considering the speed with which occupations are renewing themselves; fostering transversal key competencies which permit people to change their occupation; improving the level of technical understanding; and laying the foundations of intercultural competence which will permit people to operate in an international environment.

These are obligations imposed by international competition — but the response must take place in osmosis with the other, intrinsic, aims of education and training. Three questions thus arise: (i) how can the supreme aim of education, personal development, be fostered within a context of the quest for raising the quality of human resources in the sense in which this is intended by enterprises; (ii) how can the simultaneous acquisition of knowledge and of behaviours be promoted; and (iii) how can the uncertainty which dominates the labour market, be reduced — or at least, how can people protect themselves against labour market risks?

In order to respond to these questions, both education and training practices and those of enterprises will need to change at one and the same time. Firstly, it is necessary — for those who do so — to place less importance on filtering out the 'best brains' by selection mechanisms which are, in essence, orientated towards deductive capacities. Secondly, it is also necessary to find ways of organising pedagogy and accreditation so that the acquisition of knowledge and the acquisition of behaviours go together. From this point of view, the development and wider use of group and project based pedagogies, which are aimed to develop 'the collective can-do' appear advantageous. Lastly, it is important both that everyone acquires the capacity to exercise responsibility for their own education and training choices and that enterprises improve their capacity for predicting and managing future personnel needs.

**Innovation** permits a positive solution because it is intrinsically a value creator. The task for education systems is to develop individual capacities to solve problems; this is a capacity very different from that demonstrated by applying algorithms or any other form of pre-constructed thinking. The capacity to resolve problems is, today, the decisive capacity which enables individuals to adapt to the contemporary fast-moving world, as well as favouring the development of enterprises. Problem-solving capacity develops the learning organisation, enriches new competencies and permits the accumulation of a foundation of specific knowledge which is becoming a decisive factor of competitivity and renewal.

This implies two consequences for our education and training systems: (i) in order to place Europe appropriately in the learning society of the future, these systems must seek to shape creative persons capable of problem-solving, and (ii) in order that these persons acquire new competencies, these systems themselves must become organisms which privilege quality and innovation.

In order to move in this direction, **the Study Group recommends that Europe** should contribute to improving: (i) relations between general and vocational education and training; (ii) the definition and the comparability of acquired competencies/skills; (iii) the definition and the acquisition of new occupational profiles.

In the first instance, improving the relations between general and vocational education and training entails retention of the following principle: 'general education must provide preparation for a vocational skill, and vocational training must continue to develop the basic competencies provided by general education'.

The application of this principle leads to the following consequences for pedagogy and curricula:

- through to the close of compulsory schooling, basic competencies should be acquired in the general education system;

- teaching and learning methods should only use abstract deduction in those few areas where it seems essential and Europe must promote the best pedagogic practices that foster problem-solving;

- considerable effort should be made to develop learning about how to work in a group and to improve the accreditation of this kind of working method;

- interdisciplinarity should be developed in secondary education and at university;

- the acquisition of simple technical competencies must be made possible at all levels of general education from the onset of secondary schooling.

In organisational terms, this all leads to the following recommendations:

- whenever possible, the business sector should be significantly involved in vocational training because it does this better;

- stimulating a culture of training and learning at company level;

- but schools and teachers should concentrate on providing good quality general education, which implies that the school accepts that the business sector inserts itself into schooling in one way or another in order to effect vocational training, or at least to participate in its provision;

- the business sector and educational establishments should co-operate closely both in general education and in vocational education tracks. In an ideal system of such co-operation, 'teachers would be responsible for general education subjects in general education tracks in schools and for general education subjects within vocational training tracks organised by the business sector'. In addition, 'company trainers and other vocational trainers would be responsible for the vocational elements of general education tracks at school and for vocational training offered within the company';

- opportunities for work experience and in-company placements should be made available early on; taking such a route should allow for subsequent re-routing onto a higher education track.

In the second instance, it is necessary to facilitate personal mobility in Europe, to evaluate training systems, and to develop self-directed and lifelong learning.

These all demand that skills/competencies are defined and rendered comparable. Therefore, without seeking to establish uniform and static reglementations, it is recommended that Europe should contribute to:

- defining grid reference charts of competencies;

- introducing systems for accrediting these skills;

- making these accreditation systems widely and continuously available;

- keeping a simple ongoing check, in real time (for example, through Internet), of individual skills acquisition progress for a certain number of competencies;

- developing recognition of vocational qualifications with the use of examination procedures that involve the social partners;

- speeding up the process for modular recognition between similar courses, at least at higher education level.

In the third instance, in order to define new occupational profiles, the Study Group considers that Europe could contribute — without, of course, intending to establish a uniform reglementation — to:

- for the principal occupational sectors, identifying the new kinds of enterprises which will characterise the European economy in the next decade;

- defining a limited number of generic basic occupations which would not necessarily refer to those occupations contained in standard industrial classifications;

- developing these new definitions by bringing them into a closer relationship with present occupational classifications;

- specifying the new occupational profiles in demand for the future;

- defining the competencies to be developed for such occupational profiles, both at initial entry to employment and during active working life.

## 'Maintaining social cohesion through education and training'

To make progress, Europe needs to mobilise all its human potential: not only young people but also adults needing education and training. Europe must take care not to sacrifice the idea of developing talents and qualifications across the whole of her population to short-term exigencies. Long-term commitment to the new technological and market model which is currently establishing itself will not be achieved if it is experienced as socially unjust. In consequence, Europe must, at one and the same time, both consolidate its considerable achievements to date and put new means of integration into place.

What has been achieved comprises the will of European nations to ensure that education is democratically, and therefore easily, accessible to the largest number of people. By and large, it also includes, having given education and training systems the mission of providing the quality of opportunity to all. All European countries have affirmed these principles, which are at the heart of the social contract that exists between our societies and their education and training systems. These principles legitimate both the formation of elites and the corresponding existence of less advantageous social positions. A serious and permanent dysfunction — at this level would undoubtedly be a significant obstacle to European development, including its economic development.

In terms of the democratisation of education and training, the achievements made to date are remarkable: everywhere in Europe, rates of educational participation have risen. In contrast, genuine progress towards equality of opportunity has encountered many more difficulties. The links between social origin and formal achievement at school and university have not weakened in the last thirty years. More seriously, we are now witnessing a high degree of wastage of potential, which is reflected in high failure/drop out rates and high levels of pupil alienation — which are imputed to be related to the nature of the existing schooling system.

In order to take these phenomena into account, the Study Group considers that our education and training systems must show greater flexibility and adaptability. In order to do so, it is necessary to consolidate the dominant democratic principle which stipulates that all children have a right to universal knowledge to education, regardless of their inherent abilities, family or social circumstances. This will enable us to take better account of the growing gaps between the nature of initial circumstances and to compensate for these.

Within this perspective, the Study Group members have reached agreement on the following points: (i) it is essential to offer good quality general education to the greatest possible number; (ii) where conditions permit, the ideal would be for schools to continue to act as a social crucible, so that children from different backgrounds and circumstances have the opportunity to enjoy the same kind of education; (iii) but when the result is insufficient, more flexibility should be considered, whether in relation to specific teaching and learning methods, to specific tracks or to the question of repeating a school year; (iv) when outcomes remain unsatisfactory, we must not hesitate in envisaging specific support measures which foresee, for all pupils involved, return to the main-stream at a later date.

The Study Group affirms that the consolidation of genuine democratisation in education rests on a guarantee to all young Europeans that they will complete compulsory schooling with a foundation of recognised basic knowledge and skills.

Reinforcing the democratisation of education and promoting equality of opportunities implies the development of new means of integration. The critical points comprise: (i) pre-school education must be generally available; (ii) guidance and counselling services must enable young people to define a professional project and allow them to benefit from advice at crucial stages, that is, at the end of compulsory schooling and at university entrance; (iii) the specific treatment of the excluded who are, today, in a particularly difficult situation in that they do not posses recognised vocational qualifications; (iv) lifelong learning, which takes cognisance of the fact that learning is a continuous process, thus integrating the different aspects of education and training for given ages.

Within this overall emerging perspective, three main priority areas for European level action are discernible:

- contributing to give a guarantee at European level and for all young Europeans that they will learn and acquire a foundation of essential basic skills. This implies: (i) European-level meetings between national pro-gramme committees to define the content and nature of this foundation; (ii) wide availability of systems for the accreditation of skills; (iii) dissemination of best pedagogic practices and the promotion of manuals and multimedia tools devoted to the attainment of this objective;

- facilitating guidance and counselling at critical moments of transition, notably by placing information about generic skills and new occupational profiles at the disposition of educational establishments, together with diverse information activities;

- developing experiments that aim to support, popularise and disseminate pre-school education and the struggle against social exclusion, notably by means of pre-school and primary support outside school hours, non-formal systems of lifelong learning (notably knowledge exchange networks and the *Universités populaires*); and second chance measures, diversified in national and local contexts, which are directed to encouraging and enabling formally unqualified and socially excluded young people to return to the learning activities which are indispensable to the learning society.

Europe should be able to use its large action programmes, in particularly Leonardo da Vinci and Socrates, in order to initiate specific experiments, whilst leaving Member States to implement these on a wider scale if they so wish. These experiments could aim to disseminate good practice, in particular in pre-school education, in primary schooling and in the struggle against exclusion. An equilibrium needs to be found in the allocation of available funding, thus reserving a given proportion for highly innovative projects (about a quarter), and the remainder (about three quarters) for projects which aim to disseminate outcomes and to transfer good practice. In effect, the particularity of this proposal resides in concentrating on a number of interlinked problems at the same time, and exploring the potential for their mutual articulation.

## 'Education and training in the information society'

Undoubtedly, the exponential development of new information technologies (IT) will lead to profound transformations in education and training. Some even talk of a new paradigm which will overturn educational process and methods, educational actors' roles and positions, and even the concept of education itself. Among the potential changes identified, the following should be noted: (i) the transition from objective to constructed knowledge; (ii) the transition from an industrial to a learning society; (iii) the change in educational mission from instruction to the provision of methods for personal learning; (iv) the increasing — and perhaps, in the future, dominant — role of technology in the communication process and in knowledge acquisition; (v) the shift away from formal educational institutions such as schools and universities towards organisational structures for learning which have yet to be determined.

The Study Group considers that these developments will take place more slowly than certain current hypotheses would suppose. Technological innovations become social innovations necessarily as slowly as the capacities of organisations and individuals are able to assimilate them. Nevertheless, IT presents a considerable challenge for education and training systems. Today, many take the view that the era of school-based education is coming to a close. This will liberate educational process and will place more control in the hands of those providers that are more innovative than traditional educational structures.

The worlds of education and training must, however, take advantage of the considerable opportunity offered by these new information technologies; not only by using them, but by taking part in their development. The Study Group considers that IT provides a means to improve education: (i) by freeing teachers from numerous less central tasks, IT helps to make space for the development of more important and challenging elements of teaching practice, especially pedagogy; (ii) by improving teaching and learning methods, for example, in expanding access to data and multimedia simulations and in introducing objective assessments that are immediately accessible to the learner; (iii) by encouraging individual and small group work; (iv) by encouraging the world of education to open itself up to the community, to review its relationship with pupils and to participate in lifelong learning.

Within compulsory education it should probably be seen as complementary to traditional teaching, and in post compulsory rarely would be completely adequate alone. The policy should be to help young people to make proper use of the available technologies. The resistance to their use in public education systems probably stems from social factors and capital budget constraints rather than limitations to the current technology. The natural resistance of the traditional public system will need to be overcome by a combination of encouragement, goals, resources, consumer orientation and competition from the private sector. It might also be necessary to create, at European or national levels, a public sector virtual competitor to complement other public provision, i.e. a virtual school, college or university, at least in subjects or at levels where private sector competition is either inadequate or only available to the better-off.

As IT — understood as tools and methods and not as a 'subject' in itself — comes into more general use in mainstream education, and in the home, it is necessary to bring about changes in attitudes and to acquire the necessary equipment for schools and other such establishments. We shall also have to promote the technologies among families and with parents and young people, some of whom may find learning with less human teacher contact disconcerting. At the same time we must be vigilant as to product quality and the results obtained. Looked at from this angle, the creation at European level of a skills accreditation system will be an important means of keeping a check on the skills really being acquired via IT. Whether there is a need or 'space' for a European-wide development of educational software for 3-21 year olds but available to all ages, grounded in European culture and philosophy, and freely available as a public good, is an issue that deserves further urgent examination.

Finally, what is at stake is also important for Europe. It is doubtful whether our continent will take its rightful place in this new market if our education and training systems do not rapidly respond to the challenge. The development of these technologies, in the context of strong international competition, requires that the effects of scale play their full part. If the world of education and training does not use IT, Europe will become a mass market too late. The transformation of education and training as described earlier will then be shaped by other players.

The development and use of IT in education and training demands action on a variety of fronts, which implies that the various policy initiatives that exist in this field must be brought into co-operation with each other. The Study Group's report identifies some fifteen possible dimensions of response, which, taken together, relate to three main problems:

- the development and provision of appropriate equipment (hardware and software) for all educational levels and contexts, together with the multiplication of networking between educational establishments and resource centres (such as public libraries);

- the encouragement and support of the use of IT by teachers and trainers themselves, which entails establishing opportunities for progressive familiarisation, training and adaptation of multimedia tools;

- the fostering of innovations in learning processes themselves and for accreditation purposes, including for those competencies acquired in non-formal ways.

## 'Making education and training systems more dynamic and giving support to the actors'

The Study Group considers that if our education and training systems are to implement the suggestions made in the preceding chapters, there are five things we need to do: (i) orient the education and training systems more to users; (ii) increase productivity and effectiveness; (iii) upgrade the jobs of teacher and heads; (iv) introduce evaluation procedures both to encourage reorganisation (the 'mirror effect') and to enable users to make informed choices; (v) be more open to all forms of co-operation.

To respond to these briefly sketched imperatives, it would be desirable to draw on the abundant and valuable research conducted in recent decades on school effectiveness, school development, teaching and training methods, educational action on behalf of the disadvantaged, etc., and inform policy-makers of their findings. The dissemination of research knowledge combined with practitioner experience will permit the identification and choice of the best implementation strategies for the necessary changes.

The Study Group considers that transmitting a vision for education is more important than the general formal framework of the system itself, but it is also important to establish a fairly flexible organisation to make the vision a reality. The vision and the aim is that education should make it possible to give everyone the opportunity for personal development and for achievement at the high levels required by the new competitive economic context, and also to acquire the personal resources needed for an all-round personal development and for social integration. Modern trends indicate the need to pay more attention to the top and bottom rungs of the achievement ladder, which are both most directly affected by contemporary developments. This means we need to focus on (i) people with specialist qualifications (of whatever level) who will find themselves competing internationally with their counterparts from other regions of the world, and (ii) those who will be excluded from the learning society because they lack the resources for economic and social integration. This does not imply that those in between do not merit our attention, just that a special effort is needed on the two extremes.

Nevertheless, regardless of the organisational form and the kind of decision-making processes adopted in the different educational systems of the European Union, the objectives need to be clearly shared at European level, so that our young people know what we are trying to achieve for them. The past twenty years have seen a notable convergence of production costs, relative product prices, currencies and incomes. Yet age-specific educational targets, teaching and learning methods, curricula and assessment methods have hardly converged at all. This makes no sense. Broad-scale European initiatives are necessary here if we wish to breathe life into the European vision. It is particularly important that at the critical ages (end of compulsory schooling/ upper secondary/each university cycle) Europe specifies its aims unambiguously and informs all young Europeans where they stand personally, as well as how their school or college is performing with respect to those aims. This will ensure that our educational establishments pay greater attention to users and to their education as European citizens.

It is not easy to grasp the meaning of productivity and effectiveness in the case of education and training establishments. Any system of measurement is by definition imperfect when applied to establishments themselves. Despite all these difficulties, the Study Group considers that the efforts made in the past few years to establish productivity criteria must be continued. This trend implies support for European research on evaluation procedures and the definition of performance criteria. Europe must contribute to the implementation of these criteria by (i) relating them to clearly defined priorities based on the principles outlined with respect to the search for quality, and (ii) concentrating on the sole incontestable measure of performance, i.e. what pupils or trainees have really learned and how this impacts on their social and working life. Education and training systems will thus be more orientated towards users.

Teachers play a primordial role because they are the only people in our societies providing a service of such a marked multidimensional character. Contemporary trends are that their role is becoming even more multi-faceted, because it increasingly incorporates social, behavioural, civic, economic and technological dimensions. Teaching is an activity that can less and less be viewed from within a subject disciplinary logic, but many teachers do not have the training or experience to cope with this greatly extended role. It is clear that they should benefit from high quality pre-service teacher education.

It follows from the above that education systems will not evolve without the active participation of the basic players involved. Their everyday practice in their own establishments will change the way our systems operate. Therefore, these players must be given the appropriate means to exercise their autonomy and to find a sound balance between inducements (or pressures) and support at establishment level. Initially, then, evaluation is indispensable because it generates the information that provides — through the 'mirror effect' — a basis for continually re-evaluating one's own position. However, evaluation also has a second and equally important function. Publicly accessible, comprehensible and well founded evaluation provides a clear picture of the types of education and training available. This greater transparency is necessary so that users know what they are doing when they choose a particular field, establishment or training course. Thus, sound evaluation will greatly improve the average productivity of the education and training systems, since the learner can exercise free choice.

Therefore, the Study Group recommends focusing on the concept of 'added value' as one of the main possible guidelines for evaluation procedures. In an educational context, added value is the difference between the knowledge and skills learners possess when they enter an establishment or course, and what they possess when they leave or finish. Some Member States have set up evaluation procedures along these lines, and expanding this approach across the European Union would provide a basis for comparison. This concept of relativity is important, notably to allow teachers to alter their approaches, and the authorities to measure the return on public spending more easily.

Our education and training systems — in particular our education systems — must develop a wide range of partnerships with the other players in society. This point has been made in connection with education-industry relations. Vocational training will not develop satisfactorily without a firm partnership with companies. The same is true for social cohesion, where partnerships with local authorities and the voluntary sector are crucial.

It would also be necessary to:

- develop initial and continuing teacher education and training by the identification and discovery of best practice;

- institute a specific programme of exchanges and in-service education and training for headteachers and directors of education and training establishments;

- encourage innovative learning practices in educational establishments and training centres;

- pinpoint, study and disseminate good practice with respect to productivity and the search for quality in educational establishments and training centres;

- devise common methods for the evaluation of education and training based on experiences in national levels, in order to benefit from a comparative dimension;

- study the possibility of a legal and operational framework at European level that facilitates the development of partnerships between schools, companies and local authorities;

- look into the possibility of setting up venture capital companies to encourage the development of innovative teaching and learning products.

## 'What action should the European Union pursue?'

Article 126 of the Treaty limits the European Union's avenues of action as regards the organisation and operation of education and training systems, which clearly fall within national competence. The Study Group takes the view that this is an advantage, given the desirability of having a number of pathways to achieving similar ends. On the other hand, no interpretation of the concept of subsidiarity should be so restrictive that it prevents Europe — following discussion among the Member States and in collaboration with them — from declaring what the main common aims of our education and training systems are to be. Europe must also contribute, through initiatives and projects, to the wide dissemination of best practice and must encourage progress towards those aims. The Study Group takes the view that these efforts require more close collaboration with the Member States than has been the case to date. If we wish to lend concrete expression to the European vision that we offer to our young people and to develop lifelong learning, then education and training must be accorded a more central position in European preoccupations.

With this in mind, the guidelines for Union action on **education and training systems** could be to:

- affirm the need for the **intercultural school** to transmit the common values on which the European civilisation is founded and to assist in devising and disseminating ways of enabling the young people of Europe to play a fuller part as European citizens;

- to set as a goal the **acquisition of a foundation of essential basic knowledge at the end of compulsory education** for all young Europeans. The question of its content is open and should be the subject of joint discussion by the different Member States. This means that education and training are continuing processes that would make lifelong learning a reality;

- promote **the definition and acquisition of new occupational profiles** in which new information technologies would play a major part. Education and training systems should not try to target these precise occupations. This is not the way forward, because occupational contents change rapidly. It is better to look at what certain groups of occupations share, by the system that co-ordinates these groups, at key transversal skills that correspond and in the way which validates them;

- anchor in the Treaty or in another legal foundation **a general European aim that serves as a guide for the different systems**: such as the one proposed in this report: 'make it possible to give everyone the opportunity for personal development and to achieve at the high levels required by the new international environment and to acquire the resources needed for social integration'. The declared aim should make it clear that Europe (i) wishes to remain competitive, but (ii) will not resign itself to having an irreducible core of socially excluded persons; and (iii) wants to promote the development of the person and the education of active citizens;

- secure the financial means to achieve this goal: if we wish to see Europe placed amongst the best educational standards in the world, it will be necessary to devote a full percentage point of GDP resources in addition to that spent today. Be it initial training or continuing training, it is clear that the effort needed in all countries carries a significant cost.

# Study group on education and training

# Report

# 'Accomplishing Europe through education and training'

*December 1996*

# I. Introduction

1. Europe is today resolutely pursuing a process which is unique in its history by grouping together nations on a continent peacefully and democratically, something which some of these nations have on several occasions attempted to do by military means. This process must work to the advantage of all the peoples concerned and represent a milestone along the road of human progress. We will reach beyond the stage at which the main motivation is the avoidance of conflict between European nations, and conflict can already no longer be regarded as a legitimate response to an external threat or as a quest for domination, despite recent events in Bosnia and elsewhere. The resolve behind this voluntary process comes from within. The Union it will establish, on a bedrock of 'old' nations with solid political, social and cultural traditions, must offer an example to the world.

2. The platform first chosen to construct a 'new Europe' was an economic one, and it is on this pathway that progress has been made. The Intergovernmental Conference will achieve progress on the political front. But the success of these efforts will also depend — and perhaps especially — on the establishment of a social and human identity based on the wealth and diversity of its cultures. The common construction of this Union must represent a step forward, with the nations taking part being the prime beneficiaries. Not only will they lose nothing in this process, they will on the contrary gain from the progress of each member and from the formidable momentum which can be obtained from a democratic and stable model built by entities which have for centuries made a major contribution to the progress of human thought.

3. This is the 'European vision' the Study Group on Education and Training would like to offer our young people. This has been the Group's guiding inspiration for addressing the issues at stake in education and training. Reflecting on our education and training systems would be pointless without that vision, for we are dealing with a context in which there are too

many conflicting interests which more often than not cancel each other out. It is a context in which the jockeying for positions of power can end up failing children and adults in education and training, dashing the hopes and expectations of families, disregarding business sector needs and betraying its own lifeblood, the teachers and trainers.

## A decisive period

4.  The next 50 years will be decisive as regards where the peoples of Europe stand in the world. At a time when the population of the European Union will remain more or less stable at around 370 million, not counting enlargement (which, with the exception of Turkey, will involve countries with low rates of demographic growth), the world population will almost double and then level off more or less indefinitely, moving up from today's 5.5 billion to approximately 10 billion people, a figure which will not be exceeded until beyond the end of the 21st century. At the moment few people realise the marked asymmetry this situation will engender over the space of a generation and the manifold expectations the European populations will have to meet.

5.  These trends will be accompanied by radical changes in the composition of the populations involved. The proportion of young people in Europe is continually dwindling (the under-25s today represent 32% of the overall European population)[1] whereas in many neighbouring countries on Europe's borders they represent almost two-thirds of the population. This trend will establish itself firmly in the next two decades: population growth amongst under 20-year-olds will decrease significantly (up to 25% in Ireland) in all European Union countries with the exception of Sweden, Denmark and Luxembourg. The 117 million young people aged under 25 in the European Union are the result of new conditions, particularly in the social sphere, which have arisen in our countries: decline of the traditional peasant family, higher standards of living and better educational levels. Together, these factors result in a disinclination to have big families and improved conditions in which to foster emotional maturity, but also to the dislocation and restructuring of families, which has countervailing effects. But it will be up to these young Europeans to rise to the challenges to come, by using their skills, their creativeness, the richness of their thought, their cohesion, and the opportunity they will have to renew and update their knowledge.

---

[1] Key Data on Education in the European Union '95, Graph A1, percentages of young people aged under 25, annex 1.

## Graph A1: Percentage of under-25-year-olds, 1973, 1983 and 1993

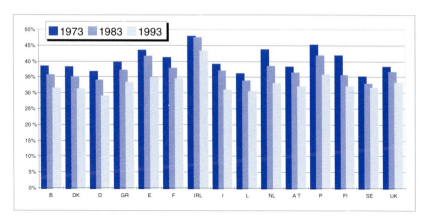

*Source:* Eurostat.

**Germany** and **Portugal**: The percentage for 1973 is an estimate.
**Germany**: The percentage for 1993 includes the new *Länder*.

6.  While these young Europeans are still the prime target of efforts to improve our education and training systems, it is also important to provide education and training to those adults who have received little education, who have not had the opportunity to realise their full potential or who need to adjust their personal and vocational skills to adapt to change through lifelong learning. The experience of the Open University — and of the various different adult education systems in Germany, France and the Nordic countries — shows that people whom the conventional education system has failed can attain high standards at undergraduate level, and, for some, beyond that. Our education and training systems, which up to now have concentrated on the young people of Europe, must continue to pursue this mission and also find new ways of opening up to the whole of the population in order to meet the needs for access to lifelong learning.

7.  This demographic asymmetry and these new social conditions come at the same time as technological upheaval and changing global relations which will bring the European population into a more direct relationship with the rest of the world's populations. Globalisation — including the dissemination of information technologies which effectively create a global synchrony of events and experiences — will unify aspirations and will shift activities even more rapidly (and very likely populations themselves, too). Trends in work/employment practices and the emergence of a learning society will be even more instrumental in defining everyone's place, as a function of skills

and knowledge built up throughout life. The nature of work itself will change as will the balance between work and leisure/culture. These changes will enhance individual responsibility in making use of the new kinds of educational facilities and possibilities that will be developed within such a society. At the same time, substantial social tensions will no doubt accompany these changes. Lastly, ever increasing ecological pressures will prompt a radical rethink of our model of economic growth, with increasing emphasis on 'sustainability'.

8. The way in which we interpret these trends will thus be decisive for a period which goes well beyond the next 50 years. Having quite rightly opted for opening out to the world, in the conviction that increasing the well-being of the most disadvantaged peoples is the best guarantee for peace (and the most powerful factor for stabilisation of demographic growth), Europe must resolutely ponder how it wishes to contribute to this new world.

9. Today's world is an uncertain one, firstly, because of the global ascendancy of a particular way of organising material life: the market, which is, by nature, a decentralised principle of allocation of resources and whose political counterpart comprises varied and changing forms of democracy. The second specific feature of uncertainty derives from the development of technological and scientific universalism which is pushing human reasoning towards infinity whilst, simultaneously, humanity's capacity to understand the world and to attain fulfilment is diminishing.

It is by no means certain that there is reason to regret those unitary visions which have sparked off the bloodiest confrontations in history. Technological progress opens up considerable prospects, including for the quality of people's lives. The system of allocation of resources used throughout the world creates emulation and competition, which must not degenerate into hysteria, and makes relations between peoples more palpably concrete. On the other hand, the current lack of human and social vision must not be allowed to continue; the human aspects such as ethics, culture, concern and caring for others, which go beyond people's lives as consumers, producers or traders, must be restored to their rightful place. This must, of course, go hand in hand with the need to restore the situation in the labour market to one of confidence in technological progress. The Study Group believes that mapping out education and training policy guidelines is a contribution to the ongoing efforts to improve competitiveness and the employment situation and, at the same time, to renew perspectives on these matters so as to confer them with a more significant ethical dimension.

# Three major requirements for an education strategy

10. The members of the Study Group, their differences of origin, nationality, occupation or culture notwithstanding, are in agreement on the following three issues:

    (i)   the need to strengthen European competitiveness in economic, technological, innovatory scientific and organisational terms. At the same time, it is well to bear in mind that competitive trade between countries and world regions is not a zero-sum game in which there are only winners and losers. Trade delivers mutual gains to all concerned. But we must better prepare our people to use their potential to the full in the global world which is taking shape. This inevitably implies solid basic training, teaching/learning methods suited to the new patterns of behaviour and the new technologies essential in the workplace, and education and training establishments capable of learning and moving with the times. The new technologies open up significant prospects, including in the world of education and training, provided we become involved in shaping them, and provided as many people as possible can have access to them and be able to use them. From this point of view, the members of the Study Group have stressed the slowness with which we are adapting our educational systems to these new demands, the lack of widespread introduction of technological innovation in schools and in teaching/learning methods, the lack of consideration given to teachers' roles and situations, and the slow development of lifelong learning. Unless a solid effort is made in this direction in order to reduce unemployment among young people, which has increased in almost all the European countries since the mid-1980s, Europe will find it increasingly difficult to retain its place and maintain its established model of social organisation;

    (ii)  the need to appreciate the difficulties of the current situation. We are witnessing a crisis in the traditional institutions of society, particularly the family and the State. These changes are likely to be accompanied by social tensions, which may be intensified in those countries with complex multi-ethnic populations. As a result of these changes, our models of authority and power are being called into question, social reference points are fading, and an individualism which is not counterbalanced by social obligations is emerging. To these features must be added: the mobility of cultures and the growth of interfaces that permit greater contact; existing multilateral mechanisms are now stretched to their limits; ethnic and religious fundamentalism; the

41

comparative poverty of some peoples; and evidence of social marginality and exclusion. All these phenomena are today making themselves felt in schools, amongst even the youngest of their pupils. In many cases the school has had to make up for the shortcomings of traditional social institutions. However, today, the scale of these shortcomings, in conjunction with the arrival of mass education makes the school's task more difficult than ever;

(iii) the need to respect the basic principles of education, whose aims go far beyond a purely utilitarian perspective. The world of education is a social crucible which educates and trains people on the basis of the knowledge and interpretations of other people and helps them to achieve self-fulfilment. In the context of the learning society, this concept can be extended to all educational activities outside school. These activities are strategic moments, with relation both to knowledge and skill acquisition and to positioning oneself in relation to others and to society. When society finds itself in a situation in which its technology and its culture are not on the same wavelength, when it can no longer see clearly ahead, then the world of education — the mirror of society itself — finds itself at a loss. In such a context, to implement ruthless changes without first assuring that people themselves are committed to them, is a step which is doomed to failure. The Study Group therefore considers that it is essential to examine just how the changes that are necessary can be put into practice.

11. The perspective that we have adopted is therefore more systemic and optimistic than normative. It comes down to considering that the current state of disordered flux is the harbinger of a new order which European society will achieve through self-reorganisation, provided that agreement can be reached on certain essential aims for education and training; that intercultural communication is developed; that the key actors can be won over and that the rigidities of systems designed to educate and train in a totally different context can be unblocked.

## Building on our heritage

12. There is an urgency to improve education and training systems, and an obligation to promote individual responsibility together with the means to exercise that responsibility in terms of acquiring and renewing one's knowledge and skills. But these current needs should not lead us to lose sight of the fundamentals of education and training. Coming back to these fundamentals facilitates an appreciation of the importance for Europe to

achieve a quantum leap in education and training, and to transcend debates over its systems.

13. **The prime aim of education and training must be the development of the whole person.** This has been stressed since the very beginnings of philosophy. It is the first element of our European heritage. This is what Aristotle says when he maintains that education must allow man to fulfil himself and find out what he truly is.[1] It is also, as Plato and later St. Augustine and the rationalists said,[2] to prompt the effort needed to get beyond human sensibility and approach an appreciation of the truth, i.e. the essence of things. It is also the way, as Erasmus stresses, to bring out the humanism carried within each individual.[3]

14. This initial idea has prompted our great thinkers to take a considered position on education, often in an authoritarian manner. Thus, for instance, in one of the founding documents of western education, 'The Republic', Plato stated that the main aim of education was to promote a just society enlightened by the highest ideals of Good. But for Plato, Good was not something which each individual could himself decide on the basis of his personal choices. Good could only be appreciated through the meta-physical doctrines which Plato sought to associate in a definitive and universal truth. On this basis, it was the philosopher himself, from his position of power, who defined the rules to be applied to the majority. Aristotle, who criticised Plato's metaphysics of Good, himself provided a more systematic metaphysics intended to achieve knowledge of being and of final causes. But he shared with Plato the conviction that education had a single purpose and that education was at the service of the aims of the state (*polis*) as a whole.

15. During the period when European cultures and institutions were generally recognised under the name of Christendom (very roughly the millennium between 700 and 1700), the metaphysical models of Greek philosophy were overtaken by Christian theology. And education was essentially considered within frontiers determined by the Church and its interests. Even the calling into question of the Church's authority during the Reformation served, for a while, to increase the authority of the Christian religion, albeit through a more divisive structure. The Christian heritage was reconstituted not on the basis of an attempt at reconciliation, but by rival

---

[1] Cf. Aristotle 'Nicomachean ethics'.

[2] Plato: 'It is necessary to see the truth in order to behave wisely in private and public life', *The Republic*, vol. VII 524d; St. Augustine: 'Words teach us only words; even less than that, a sound and a mere voice... it is therefore the knowledge of things which enables the knowledge of words', *De magistro*.

[3] Erasmus: 'De libero arbitrio diatribe'.

and antagonistic orthodoxies through which each sought to push forward its sphere of influence by exerting painstaking control over the doctrine. Equally, control over education and training was on a greater scale than had been the case during the humanist period of the Renaissance. Schooling was extended to larger numbers of the population and many of the internal organisational features of the modern school were designed at that period.

16. Despite the authoritarian tradition and rigorous discipline through which metaphysical concepts and educational ideals of the churches were transmitted, many worthwhile values and virtues were carried forward as part of the European heritage. Some of the classical and religious ideals of European education, whether as 'knowledge' or 'belief', have served as vehicles for a deep-rooted — if not always practised — conviction. This conviction is that human beings have an incomparable value, that their lives, social relations and spiritual development can be greatly enriched by education. These classical and religious ideals see such enrichment as the best way to achieve originality and societal creativity. The life and works of Erasmus illustrate the potential of this conviction.

17. The 17th century witnessed the rise of modern scientific epistemology and methodology, particularly associated with figures such as Galileo, Francis Bacon and Isaac Newton and with the many scientific societies and institutes which started to flourish in the main European centres of knowledge. One of the main consequences of this trend was that theology lost its status as the supreme form of knowledge and that metaphysics no longer represented the sole truth.

18. The methodological scepticism of thinkers such as René Descartes (1596–1650) and David Hume (1711–1776) weakened the authoritarian concepts of an education founded in metaphysics. Many critical currents of this type emerged during the Enlightenment. Rousseau's treatises on education and Kant's analysis of the potential of human reason provided the most disturbing ideas of the time.

19. The French and American revolutions were very largely the political results of the Enlightenment and they mark the transition between Christendom and modernity. With the generalisation of a scientific and universalist spirit, a decisive step had been taken. Henceforth, reason must overcome the artificial barriers which had been placed between humanity and the rest of the universe. First and foremost, human beings must recognise that they do not stand at the centre of that universe. They must, instead, seek rational knowledge. This quest will be the spur for the development of

human reasoning. The rational spirit accepts all hypotheses, organises, classifies, experiments and theorises in the most general way possible. It enables humanity to develop through exercising reason, and human fulfilment can be achieved by access to rational knowledge and the methods by which such knowledge is consolidated and transmitted. Thus, education has a fundamental vocation to transmit knowledge and provide the methods for building on it.

20. In addition, fuller recognition of the role of the arts and all cultural activities took place at about the same time. The permanence of artistic, literary and musical creation, which build bridges between very different universes, was acknowledged. Mozart's work during the Enlightenment upheavals is an example. It was also acknowledged that these activities were necessary for creativeness, and could at the same time give rise to new values, including economic values. The conditions for the development of the person were, then, generally accepted. These conditions include rational reason, the methodological competence to access knowledge, and an artistic and cultural curiosity conferring hindsight and creativity. Together, they open the way towards a genuine understanding of the world and its phenomena.

21. The recognition that education as a means of socialisation on a mass scale is an obligation emerged in the midst of these developments. This was the result of the development of the social sciences and of the in-depth analysis of social phenomena. It was also the result of the need to consolidate the great nation states (which were often at war with one another). And, finally, it was the result of the industrial revolution, which required a literate and numerate workforce. The idea of education for all was introduced, together with the idea that education belongs in the public sphere. Thus, education systems were born.

22. **It was at this point that the second major aim of education emerged: socialisation.** The resolve to 'make reasoning popular' we owe to Condorcet, who called on state and public authorities to commit themselves to this aim: 'Friends of equality and liberty! Unite in your efforts to make the public authorities provide an education which makes reasoning popular'.[1] Education should target everyone, irrespective of gender, ethnicity and social class. It should distinguish between general basic education, vocational education and research. Moreover, this education concerns not only children; it must include continuing education as well. This is the origin of lifelong learning. Subsequently, the school's sociali-

---

[1] Condorcet, 'Cinq mémoires sur l'instruction publique', 1791.

sation role was underlined still further: education and training were expected to fashion the citizen of our nation states, to provide equal opportunities by combatting social reproduction, and to promote access to knowledge and to employment.

23. The national education systems that were established in many European countries in the 19th century sparked off recurring conflicts between state and church. However, those who fought for control of national education policies seldom had a less interventionist attitude than the religious authorities of previous centuries.

24. It was not until the start of the 20th century that the vision of the Enlightenment really took hold in national education systems. One of the important reasons is that the twentieth century became the moment at which the needs of the child became a conscious issue. These developments were based on a progressive education tradition dating back to Rousseau through Pestalozzi and Froebel, culminating in the ideas of John Dewey. The publication in 1900 of the Swedish educationalist Ellen Key's 'The Century of the Child' is an example of work in this tradition.

This tradition prompted the recognition of two principles with numerous implications. The first implication is that pupils or learners must be considered as active subjects responsible for their own learning. The second implication is that teachers' or trainers' methods should be directed towards gradually getting the best out of pupils or learners. At this point, it was truly recognised that children must not merely acquire skills, qualifications and influences. They must also develop their own personalities by taking part in different activities tailored to each person's possibilities and limitations. This also implies a specific effort to uncover and foster the latent individual attributes and talents which contribute to the shaping of personal identity. The 20th century has seen a truly remarkable achievement in these respects, in making primary and secondary schooling a universal experience and, over the past thirty years, in bringing further and higher education within reach of significant proportions of the population.

25. This brief historical account of the main contributions made by certain educational thinkers shows that subsequent developments have gathered pace. The organisational principles of our education systems are certainly different between the Member States. Some may place emphasis on public education/training provision and the role of the state; elsewhere individual responsibility plays a greater role and the autonomy of education and training establishments is more clearly defined. In certain countries

stress has been laid on general education and training provided in academic institutions; in other countries the business sector or local authorities have played an important part.

26. However, there is much in common. Denominational systems have held their own everywhere; and almost everywhere in Europe, education and training are, by and large, dominated directly or indirectly by the public authorities. The idea that education should be provided in the general interest also applies to the production and dissemination of educational products based on new technologies and their mode of transmission. Even when products such as educational multimedia are intended for the market, they are expected to comply with the notion of the general interest or a universal service. Everywhere, education establishments are required to foster personal development, to help the formation of citizens, to mediate and promote knowledge, to socialise men and women with the aim of combatting social reproduction, and to prepare people for employment. And everywhere, education and training establishments — which have already contributed to a substantial rise in educational standards amongst the European populations — are now confronted with increasing and more diversified demands. The momentum has accelerated and intensified: education and training establishments must now simultaneously satisfy all the fundamental aims established by the thinkers quoted earlier — and on a greater scale than ever before.

27. The acceleration and intensification that has taken place can be clearly seen when we look at changes in education and training contents. It has taken several centuries to establish the universal right to general education. The recognition that everyone needs to obtain a vocational qualification dates back only to the 1980s. The current period is one of the development of autonomous and fully-rounded persons, who possess key competencies founded on basic knowledge and social skills. These social skills include, in particular, methods for learning with a view to adaptability, being conversant with information technologies, communication skills, the capacity to work as part of a team and to develop partnerships as well as to take individual responsibility. The speed at which these skills are being introduced into work organisations, in particular multinationals, is outpacing the capacity of our education and training systems to produce people who possess and can use them. And although things have improved considerably, our education and training systems are out of step because society is moving ahead faster than they are.

28. In the recent past, the two fundamental aims noted earlier — the development of the person and socialisation — have been joined by **a third aim: personal and vocational preparation for entering a complex, demanding and rapidly changing economic world.** At all levels of the educational system, the emphasis placed on vocationalism has significantly modified educational content, with the introduction of technical subjects and a clearly affirmed will to provide young people with the knowledge and skills that facilitate a smoother transition to working life. Labour market tensions have served to accentuate this trend. Post-school vocational training programmes have been established with the aim of furnishing young people — but also the adult unemployed — with the vocational preparation necessary to accede to employment.

## Different routes to a common aim

29. The proposal for a European vision for young people must obviously go further than this. It is in education and training that values take shape and are transmitted to the next generation — particularly the ideals of peace, safety and tolerance. It is there that people learn to practice these values through democratic choice. It is also where, essentially, people acquire a social conscience, respect for success and compassion with failure. Lastly, it is in this context that people gain the qualifications and skills to meet the challenges of the new world.

30. There is evidence that the prime aims of education and training — i.e. personal development, educating and training the citizen, socialisation, enhancing employability and the capacity to create self-employment — can be reconciled. Changes in occupations, the speed of technological change and the need for creativity and innovation are calling out for basic aptitudes and the capacity for renewal; these can be obtained through general and vocational education and training. How can we fail to see that? How can we fail to understand that the consolidation and transmission of common values will be a decisive factor of integration for our continent? Can anyone doubt that success in the fight against social exclusion and in achieving a higher degree of social cohesion will bring the 'European social model' back to the forefront on the international scene? How can anyone fail to see that if we can turn new technologies to the advantage of lifelong education and training, then Europe will be able to recoup its position vis-à-vis the United States and Asia and once more become one of the pivots of future developments?

31. Contrary to what might be assumed, the plurality of convictions, pathways and institutions will not be an obstacle provided everyone agrees on a clear and common goal. As several members of the Study Group have pointed out, the only certainty we have is that nothing is certain. Europe does not have an uncontested, single social or human 'model' that offers itself as a goal and which could inform the essential purposes of education and training. Furthermore, intangible 'toolboxes' are no longer available as guidelines for teaching and learning from one generation to the next. But what Europe does have is a diversity which, if properly harnessed, should enable it to provide essential ethical references and the fundamental knowledge and the vocational aptitudes which would enable its people both to find their way in life and to be able to debate the models of society and of citizenship that they would variously like to promote and build. Europe can better rise to the new challenges by organising a process of change rather than by transmitting prespecified models of social and economic life.

32. The Study Group has focused its attention on how best to assemble these assets. Europe can take a decisive step towards consolidating its rallying values by identifying the values we all want to hand down to our children and examine how these values can be profitably introduced into our educational and training systems. Europe can give credibility to a European vision founded in a broadly consensual concept of social cohesion. It can do so by using all possible means to reduce the effects of disadvantage and disability, to maximise knowledge and skills, and to enhance people's confidence in themselves — and to do all this for everyone, in the classroom. Effects of scale are also applicable to the education and training context. In making use of these effects, Europe can take full part in the technological challenge and in the production of more intangible and intelligent new market values. On this count, we would do well to reflect on the cost of **not** realising the European dimension of education and training, in much the same way as this was calculated some 15 years ago for the economic sphere.

33. It is by consciously getting things moving at EU level — which must play its full role of lending impulse and diffusing good practice — and at national level that these steps forward can be achieved, with the support of measures taken at European Union level. The point is to build up real partnerships between the educational players and the business and industrial players, particularly companies and the social partners, local authorities and associations. This implies recognition of how important it is to have education and training systems which function efficiently and move with the times. It also implies toning down corporatism and

preventing the real complexity of education and training issues being used as pretexts to consolidate the most conservative points of view.

34. As the 20th century draws to a close, Europe is entering a new era in its educational history, that of lifelong learning. The EU has proclaimed 1996 as the European Year of Lifelong Learning in order to fuel discussion on how to rise to the challenges we face. These challenges are also the focus of the European Commission's recently-published White Paper '*Teaching and learning: towards the learning society*'. Establishing a genuine learning society will require major changes in our education and training establishments. The Study Group considers that the changes in education and training systems should concern four principal directions which comprise the aims to attain between now and the year 2000. From this perspective, the orientations for action envisage: (i) constructing European citizenship, (ii) reinforcing European competitiveness and preserving employment, (iii) maintaining social cohesion in Europe, (iv) fully utilising the opportunities offered by the Information Society. In conclusion, the report considers implementation issues by looking at how our education and training systems operate and at the players involved, particularly teachers and heads of educational establishments.

# II. Constructing European citizenship through education and training

## European citizenship: an original idea but early days yet

35.   European citizenship is an essentially humanistic idea designed to construct a democratic Europe that is respectful of a balance between economic, technological, ecological and cultural considerations. The 'European vision' is one in which our nations learn to live together and to settle their disputes without seeking 'foreign scapegoats'. Yesterday's European nightmare was the Holocaust, today's is 'ethnic cleansing'. Introducing the idea of a European citizenship — as Article 8 of the Maastricht Treaty indisputably does — has significant implications, in that it goes beyond an economic approach to European integration, accords the Member States the role of actors in the process of the construction of such citizenship, consolidates existing citizenship rights and institutes new rights.

36.   So the mission is to muster the people of Europe to take on one of the greatest challenges of all time: to construct a greater Europe, within a continent that is characterised by cultural differences, differing economic approaches and varying natural environments, but which is also united by a feeling of belonging to a common civilisation. For the first time, European integration will not be the result of political or military hegemony imposed by a dominating power. Rather, it will be the outcome of the steady progress of democratic decision-making processes. A clearer perception of the meaning of the project will be the basis of that progress, which will gather momentum as we prove ourselves capable of accepting a common set of rules and behavioural principles, while not necessarily sharing the same values. It is within this framework that individuals will feel free to pursue their own aims.

37.   This process of European integration does not require a choice between the institutional systems 'most typical' of the different nations. Rather, it is

based on **a shared political culture of democracy** — and it is this that Europe, at its best, can offer to the rest of the world. This is the route towards a 'post-national' model of Europe to which Europeans will feel they belong as citizens, not because they subscribe to a common culture (which cannot, in any case, be imposed) or because of their specific origins, but because this sense of citizenship will emerge from the new social relations that Europeans establish between themselves.

38. Europe can thus rise to the huge challenge of 'living together' in a context of individual and collective freedom (of cultural diversity). In such a context, majority rule, which is the linchpin of democratic institutions, must take due account of the legitimate expression of differences, but should not be placed under permanent pressure from those differences. The most valuable lesson that a democratic regrouping of European nations can offer the world is perhaps the experience of learning, in our daily practice, that the values each of us holds to be universal may be more particularistic than we believe. It is through tolerance, which has perforce to be learned, that we become capable of distilling non-contradictory and mutually acceptable values. On that basis, we can co-operate with each other and Europe, caught up in global competition, can then maintain a level of solidarity that is sufficiently in keeping with the spiritual foundation of its humanist values. At the same time, Europe can thus develop an open and continuous global dialogue with other peoples and cultures.

39. This is the road we are walking along today. It is important for Europeans, particularly young people, to realise what is at stake and take a responsible part in the debates and the choices to be made. If education and training fail to lend impulse to this debate — which is well underway among intellectuals — then the new Europe will pursue its reconstruction in complete contradiction with its own democratic principles. The process of integration will enjoy no popular support and will be seen to have been imposed from above. The result will consequently be fragile.

The new European citizenship thus needs to be considered in terms of taking account of the decline in Eurocentrism and its implication, in a multicultural context, of opening up to global cultures against the background of the weakening — perhaps implosion — of nation-states and the need to overcome the crisis in our systems of political representation. This new concept must provide European citizens with the means to situate themselves within the construction of the Information Society and the globalisation of trade. And it must equip our societies with the tools to reinforce the struggle against social exclusion and to deal with the weakening — perhaps disintegration — of traditional socialisation agencies.

# Going through the motions is not enough

40. Citizenship is not simply a collection of behavioural principles founded on common values and norms. If the aim is to lend citizenship an identifiable content, one that people will want put into to practice, then we must go further. Citizenship is a multi-faceted idea: it is to be understood as a social practice, as a normative idea, and as a relational practice. It also has democratic, egalitarian, intercultural and ecological dimensions.

41. Individuals and groups can be included in and excluded from different aspects of citizenship, in varying degrees. In other words, they possess different citizenship statuses. Social inequalities regulate and differentiate modalities of access to citizenship. In addition, the different aspects of citizenship do not necessarily co-exist in a straightforward manner. They may stand in conflict with one another. The 'embryonic' citizenship of the EU is a good example: legal rights to mobility are not accompanied by political rights to full electoral participation.

42. But even when different aspects of citizenship do, in some measure, co-exist, some groups, in particular young people, can be seen as 'foreigners in their own societies'. Their access to citizenship is restricted initially on the grounds of their age, which is held to indicate lack of maturity and responsibility. More importantly, however, young people's access to citizenship is constrained because of the breakdown of established mechanisms and routes of transition to independent adult life. Their citizenship status is ambiguous as a result of prolonged dependency upon their families and/or the welfare state. These kinds of problems are particularly acute for highly marginalised/excluded youth, who can hardly sense themselves to be full citizens.

43. Citizenship is also closely related to the kind of society and polity we want to live in: citizenship is thus a normative idea. Contemporary democratic citizenship is therefore allied to the concept of civil society and its moral/ideological defence. This aspect of citizenship speaks to the identities and values held by political communities, i.e., cultural/ethnic groups and nations/states. It emphasises the sense of belonging that develops from shared circumstances and experiences: people become committed to a set of values and norms; they feel a sense of responsibility towards each other and towards the community to which they all contribute. With the construction of a 'new Europe', citizenship accretes a new space for expression, a space that inserts itself into existing ideas of citizenship but does not replace them.

44. Citizenship is thus a dynamic notion that evolves in a dynamic process, in which the sense of belonging is shaped through differences, communication with others, conflicts and negotiated compromises, and mutual images. But a non-negotiable foundation remains: democratic human rights. All the evidence we have confirms that most people in Europe attach great importance to these fundamental values, even though there may be a disjunction between their principles and their practices. In this respect, differences certainly exist according to social and cultural context, but on closer inspection, it is more a matter of the practical interpretation of the principles concerned. Disjunctions between democratic principles and practices are not, therefore, the province of particular social or age groups.

45. Finally, citizenship is located at the structural and interactional interfaces between the individual, the state and the community. It is therefore a political practice whose terrain of development is people's social situation and political participation. Active citizenship demands the acquisition of cognitive and communicative competence through social and educative process. Access to active citizenship requires the human rights noted earlier. However, education plays an important role in the promotion of active citizenship. This role can be played out in the context of formal educational institutions, but equally in primary and peer groups, in the community, and through the mass media. Citizenship education does already exist in most Member States: but under different names and for different purposes, for different amounts of time and for different ages and pupil groups — and the European dimension of citizenship is very underdeveloped, which is not surprising, given that European citizenship is an ambiguous, contradictory conceptual space. [1]

## A central issue: gender relationships

46. The Study Group considers that feminist critique of androcentric perspectives on citizenship and human rights is a model to show how we can learn to place apparently universal values into relational perspective without falling into a moral void. [2]

---

[1] Each time young people organise a 'project café' for local kids, whilst others put a refuse collection and recycling campaign into action, and yet again others — coming from four different countries — prepare an anti-racist public event and tour round European cities and villages to put it on show, they are all learning active citizenship and putting it into practice in daily life, and for the most part, doing so in a multicultural society.

[2] Gender and citizenship is a topic that is currently attracting considerable interest. The Commission has recently published a report entitled Women and European Citizenship (by E. Vogel-Polsky, J. Vogel and V. Degraef; DGV/233/94, Brussels).

47. In the first place, women were forced to struggle for the right to fully-fledged citizenship. It was a long and fraught struggle,[1] marked in turn by progress and setbacks. Before the French revolution public political life was exclusively dominated by male heads of households, who, in taking part in civil society, took on the role of citizen. Locke extended citizenship rights to all men, not only those who were fathers, i.e. heads of a household. Inspired by the French Revolutionary period and in response to Thomas Paine's 'The Rights of Man' (1791), Mary Wollstonecraft published her 'Vindication of the Rights of Women' in 1792. In this tradition, Condorcet rationally and openly called for women to be considered as fully-fledged citizens. J. Stuart Mill in particular also figured prominently as a champion of the women's cause. Following an eventful history, a genuine politics in favour of the emancipation of women established itself from about 1870. Associations, action leagues and political periodicals were established (especially in France, the UK and Italy) in order to obtain political and civic rights for that half of the population which was denied them. In 1906, Finland was the first European country to extend voting rights to women, but it was not until the end of the First World War that women in Great Britain obtained the right to vote (1919), a breakthrough which came much later in France and in Italy (1945) as a sort of reward after the suffering of the war periods.

48. This brief historical sketch shows that the entry of women into the public arena was considered as simply an expansion of the electorate. It was not understood then that the point was to rethink democracy and its principles by amending certain basic parameters. The problem was to define the new principles and the new rights which democracies should adopt and defend, now that they had a new group of members altogether. Thus, despite formal recognition of women's rights, numerous kinds of covert and structural discrimination could develop, founded on analyses of fundamental gender differences. Some analyses focused on biological and physical/bodily differences. Others identified the difference in an opposition between a 'feminine ethic of caring' opposed to a 'masculine ethic of the pursual of interest'. Still others pointed to an opposition between 'responsibility' and 'rationality', the latter, of course, considered a male prerogative. Even if these differences might, at first sight, be flattering for women, they nonetheless contain the seeds of subtle discrimination, for instance as regards the capacity of women to be engineers, scientists or leaders.

---

[1] The feminist Olympe de Gouges (*The Declaration of Women's Rights*) was guillotined during the French revolution. She was declared guilty of opposing the natural division of gender roles, having claimed the right to hold formal political office.

49. Today the facts are there. Despite formal equality in principle, all too few women are to be found in elected assemblies, top positions and scientific and engineering professions. We now know that formal principles alone do not secure equality in practice, whether in education or in the workplace; that equality is a very complex matter altogether; and that gender inequalities arise, above all, from the differential positioning of women and men in the public **and** the private spheres of social life. Education and training are not exempt from all this, for even if the law has changed, the legacy of old-fashioned ideas is hard to shake off. Worse, such ideas have been tacitly accepted at school by teachers and even pupils themselves. Girls and young women often out-perform boys and young men. But the role of teachers is fundamental, both to avoid the transmission of stereotypes and to valorise the advantages of co-education. The aim should be to promote girls' and boys' potential equally, and to employ new methods with this in mind.

50. So it is not enough to proclaim an abstract right. To make headway, education and training must become a positive ally in making progress towards European citizenship, based on **the fundamental principle that education and training must destroy all stereotypes of human beings.**

There are five essential dimensions to a new citizenship:

- the dignity and centrality of the human person; the knowledge of democratic political institutions; majorities and minorities in the democratic governance of peoples; media which can express themselves freely but are fully conscious of their responsibilities;

- social citizenship: social rights and responsibilities; the struggle against social exclusion and marginalisation; solidarity as an intrinsically European achievement; social cohesion and the reinforcement of community spirit;

- egalitarian citizenship: rejection of discrimination and prejudice based on gender and ethnicity; understanding the value of equality; equality of opportunity across the board in education;

- intercultural citizenship: the value of diversity and openness for a plural world; European identity and multiculturalism; respect for different cultures and the legitimate expression of collective rights; tolerance and the active search for the richness of difference; European and global 'good neighbourliness';

- ecological citizenship: the preservation of the ecosystem; rapprochement between humanity and nature; accreted conscience of environmental values; the key significance of sustainable development.

## What should Europe be doing?

51. The Study Group thinks that Europe should play a role through education and training: (i) to affirm and transmit the common values on which its civilisation is founded; (ii) to assist in devising and disseminating ways of enabling the young people of Europe to play a fuller part as European citizens; (iii) to identify and disseminate best practice in education and training for citizenship, in order to filter out the best means of learning contemporary elements of European citizenship and especially, to develop these methods.

52. The main values the Study Group considers as part of Europe's inalienable heritage are values oriented towards the future, not values that are the lines of defence of our civilisation. This is the basis for a progressive version of the learning society which is now taking shape. In such a society, principles of justice and solidarity can be respected, which will permit shared knowledge, the best remedy against intolerance in our nations. These values are:

---

- human rights/human dignity
- fundamental freedoms
- democratic legitimacy
- peace and the rejection of violence as a means to an end
- respect for others
- a spirit of solidarity (within Europe and vis-à-vis the world as a whole)
- equitable development
- equal opportunities
- the principles of rational thought: the ethics of evidence and proof
- preservation of the ecosystem
- personal responsibility

---

53. These values obviously have to be taught if they are to become a practical reality. This is what the official curricula of European countries seek to promote today, whether for under 16s or for 16-18-year olds. Some devote a comparatively small number of hours (1-2 hours weekly over the year) to

civic education, while others see this topic as part of history or social science subjects, and yet others consider these values as underlying guidelines for educational process as a whole. A closer look at the content of what is taught shows fairly substantial differences, which is partly explained by varying degrees of 'patriotic' choices in the selection of the historical periods covered and the topics that are included. The idea of Europe finds a place in all countries' curricula, but more as an institutional system than as a construction process. This latter approach is patently a fruitful one for developing new forms of co-operation. When the content of civic and social education is devised on truly educational lines, with sound theoretical bases, and where the methodology of teaching promotes active learning and engagement by the pupils, the subject is of great benefit in fostering good citizenship. To achieve this, the approach must avoid any tendencies towards chauvinism and indoctrination.

54. Given both the general overload of primary and secondary school syllabi, **and** the need for curricular changes that will permit fuller development of foreign language teaching and learning (a decisive factor in the construction of European citizenship), the Study Group considers that to recommend an increase in the number of contact hours for civic education or the creation of specific curricula on Europe is too costly and too formal an approach. The results could be very disappointing in relation to the resources required.

55. It would be a better option to:

- study in detail the key facts of discrimination among citizens, particularly those relating to the issues of gender and inter-ethnic relations,

- promote university research on these issues,

- highlight European achievements in the arts and sciences as a common heritage for all citizens, and thus the transnational character of their influence and importance,

- in the teaching of history, social science or literature, present analyses on the main areas of social, political and ethnic conflicts which lead to violence in Europe itself and in Europe's bordering regions. These analyses could be tackled by pupils as group projects and used as a basis for discussing the basis for common identity and mutual solidarity between European citizens founded in common values and heritage.

56. Rather than consider extra courses, or a revamping of the curriculum which might involve specialised teacher-training, the Study Group recommends developing training courses on Europe for those teachers directly concerned, and more opportunities for headteachers to benefit from mobility between European countries. Europe is an excellent level at which to address the citizenship issues of today. It is by introducing citizenship issues into those subject areas most closely connected to them (particularly history, philosophy, social sciences, literature, the arts and music) that young minds have the opportunity to form their own opinion about these issues and their ongoing development.

57. Education and training for active citizenship is not only a matter of transmitting values. **It is perhaps especially a question of methods.** Approaches to teaching and learning are crucial in this context, and a specific pedagogy for citizenship needs to be developed. The Study Group considers that there is a need to encourage all active pedagogies, which are based on a fostering critical awareness, independence of reasoning and group work. The application of these new approaches also entails changes in assessment and accreditation methods. A course on citizenship should not be used as a means of checking the pupil's ability report, changes in teaching and learning methods in the directions proposed above are equally significant for acquiring appropriate personal and social skills that are demanded in today's workworld. Labour market competitiveness can therefore be enhanced by encouraging a well-developed sense of citizenship.

58. Education for active citizenship is essentially a question of education for individual empowerment. This means, above all, developing people's critical faculties and the ability to make considered judgements through learning to analyse and understand one's own life circumstances and value positions in comparison with those of other individuals and groups. The skills involved here are analogous to research skills, in particular, those practised in modern ethnography or as developed through intercultural education. Most simply, these skills involve making the familiar strange and the strange familiar: being able to switch between standpoints and identity positions, and between empathy and critical distance. Learning these skills is to some extent a matter of using techniques and of training observational-analytical capacities; but it is also a matter of having the confidence to switch position — in particular, to regard oneself critically and to tolerate personal and social ambiguities and contradictions. The idea of 'border pedagogy' is one significant attempt to catch what is meant by education for empowerment. Crossing borders (one's own, those of others, internal vs. external borders) is a core skill for European

citizens, during which people can gain the confidence to see differences as positive opportunities for.communication and mutual understanding. In addition to the crucial role of this kind of pedagogy for intercultural communication and understanding, it is clear that it can also play a role in learning to perceive, understand and thus to gain a measure of autonomy over media messages. Media education has an important role to play in developing border pedagogy as a practical tool for teaching and learning. Both traditional media (for example, written policy documents) and the new IT media (especially the highly visual forms) offer new opportunities for learning how to look critically at the construction of images, representations and texts and their 'hidden messages'.

59. Summing up these different points, the Study Group has identified the main tasks facing schools, as the public sphere of action and of education for active citizenship, in putting 'citizens' schools' into action. It is necessary to:

- improve knowledge of foreign languages and understanding of European cultures; [1]

- modernise the curricula and teaching of history, geography (notably by encouraging the production of European textbooks), philosophy and social sciences with respect to providing all pupils in our schools with an understanding and valorisation of a common vision of European achievements. This equally implies a process of 'disarmament' of educational content insofar as its elements have been inspired by warfare and violent events, as well as — in the interests of justice — denouncing historical 'facts' that are in reality discriminatory. This modernisation process should affirm the driving force of ideas as well as the importance of the equal contributions of scientific thought and the paths taken by the humanities, literature and the arts in Europe. The common aim would thus be the formation of the measured and impartial judgement of human action and progress, including the errors made along the way;

- support democratic styles of educational governance and models of leadership open to strong community involvement;

---

[1] The learning of one or more foreign languages is general to secondary education in the European Union. In Ireland, this is still not a compulsory part of the curriculum. In almost half of the Member States (Belgium, Germany, France, Luxembourg, The Netherlands, Austria, Finland and Sweden), learning a third language is possible, even obligatory. In 1992/3, 88% of pupils in general secondary education were learning English as a foreign language. Other foreign languages were chosen significantly less often: 32% were learning French, 19% German, and only 9% Spanish.

- invest solidly in the training of teachers and directors of establishments and support the implementation of genuinely intercultural teaching strategies;

- the Study Group considers that lifelong education is an incontrovertible challenge, which implies a capacity to be able to access full citizenship, understood here to comprise the development of a firm civic conscience, methods of continuous learning, the means of participating in community life and the willingness to participate in the project of constructing Europe.

60. Education and training obviously cannot achieve all this by itself. Co-operation with other actors will be necessary, in particular with local authorities and associations, which are key contexts for the practical implementation of citizenship. This co-operation implies that education and training establishments recognise and use the competencies that other players have to offer. This also means that administrative staff become more directly involved in local community life.

61. The best way to learn about citizenship is to put it into practice at school. This presupposes styles of management that are conductive to democratic pupil life. This does not mean the delegation of school management to pupils, nor that pupils necessarily oppose their 'managers'. It means that issues which concern them, particularly in their relationships with one another, should be directly addressed by them. The Study Group therefore suggests that experiences in developing the intercultural school should be brought together and examined at European level. This kind of school does not need to be invented: it already exists, both in the upper classes of international schools and in the schools of multiethnic neighbourhoods. And it is in schools — but in general everywhere — that Europe needs to organise pilot projects, in close collaboration with the Member States. The intercultural school epitomizes the whole issue of citizenship, and it should become a test-bed for working in the kind of social and educational context that will become more widespread in Europe in the future, both due to the demographic trends described earlier and in the light of the progress to be made in building a new Europe.

62. In order to promote the idea of the 'intercultural school', the following features are proposed as a checklist for action:

- **Target**: in the first instance, schools in multiethnic neighbourhoods whose pupils come from a wide spread of cultural origins, and subsequently in all schools.

- **Curriculum**: normal with greater emphasis on the historical content around the cultures represented; civic education, history of European democracy and contemporary historical relations between Europe and the other regions and cultures of the world. Appropriate application of the White Paper objective of having two languages (not necessarily Community languages) in addition to the national language, with a learning approach which takes on board interculturality.

- **Pedagogy**: focus on active teaching and learning methods and group work, systematic use of border pedagogy, but with a simultaneous check on the acquisition of basic knowledge. Experimentation with more inductive methods in classical core curriculum areas.

- **Teaching staff**: open to the active participation of parents and local community workers.

- **Civil life in the classroom**: civil charter, internal procedure for settling disputes, solidarity drives, establishment — as a legal entity — of a democratically-functioning association in line with the traditions of the countries and communities represented.

- **School management**: attainment requirements identical to those for pupils elsewhere, same rules, headteacher and class teachers trained in to practice intercultural pedagogy.

# III. Reinforcing European competitiveness and preserving employment through education and training

## The constraints of competitiveness

63. The threats today hanging over European competitiveness are seriously underestimated. Despite substantial efforts as regards production costs, product quality, technological and organisational innovation, Europe is facing very stiff competition in terms of both low and high qualifications. The relative level of monetary parities in those countries most active in support of monetary union has undoubtedly played a major part in industrial job losses seen in Europe. By the same token, the high degree of substitution of capital for labour observed in certain countries has reached a scale unjustified by the respective levels of salaries and the cost of capital. Today, Europe is lagging behind its competitors and unemployment rates are too high — but it would be absurd to argue that this state of affairs is solely due to the shortcomings of Europe's education and training systems.

64. The information society is set to expand the possibilities for using skilled labour in non-European countries at costs well below those applicable in Europe. European companies operating on a world scale are quick — and will continue to be quick — to seize these opportunities in order to maintain their positions, or simply to survive, which is their main long-term concern. This is not something that can be solved by introducing regulations, partly because the most visible consequence of the trend is that salaries and social conditions are rising to meet European levels in those countries that today compete with Europe on the basis of lower wage levels. The cost of labour in Japan in the past 30 years has caught up with the average cost of labour in Europe; several other newly industrialised countries show similar trends. Europe cannot, therefore, avoid this issue if it wants to stay in the race.

65. In the light of this, and despite the considerable efforts that have been made in education and training reforms to date, the Study Group takes the view that education and training systems are insufficiently aware of the constraints of competitiveness. Yet their crucial responsibility is incontestable: it is education and training that must disseminate knowledge and provide our young people with a sufficient level of skills, qualifications and aptitudes which will put us in a position to meet this challenge. The main valid long term option to allow Europe to survive and remain competitive on foreign markets is to have **a high capacity for quality and innovation.**

66. We are not adjusting quickly enough to the new technological challenges and to the new economic environment. The assets education and training in Europe can assemble are invaluable from this point of view, provided the systems can adapt to economic and technological change. In the context of profound socio-economic changes, a conservative system will find it difficult to produce innovative individuals. The conclusion of IRDAC's latest report can be applied to both education systems and the business sector: 'there is a need to extend awareness of the implications of industrial change within European citizens, to promote the concepts of innovation and quality within the European economy, and to make sure that industry and education deliver fast and flexible responses to new demands'.[1]

67. The features of the 21st century company must be taken into account by education and training systems. This company will very likely be:

- generally open to the outside (multinationals, of course, but also SMEs),

- largely organised around information technologies, either within an internal network, or as part of an inter-company network,

- flexibly structured and capable of adjusting rapidly around 'profit centres', composed of project teams,

- faced with very stringent standards in terms of quality and respect for the environment,

- concerned by a high degree of product diversification which will imply increasing use of design, fashion, art and culture,

---

[1] *'Quality and relevance'*, IRDAC (Industrial Research and Development Advisory Committee of the European Commission), 1994, p. VII.

- placed in a technological context with a very short life cycle, which implies a need for permanent change to allow for adaptability, innovation, learning, and development of basic skills.

68. These features of industry are accompanied by the development of the services sector and of self-employment, which also increasingly require quality, innovation and communicative capacity. Even though many of today's jobs are still routine and repetitive, the Study Group considers that education and training adjustments must be oriented to the needs of our economic front line, i.e. big or small companies facing up to international competition. At the same time, changing circumstances mean that many people today are increasingly called upon to find ways of combining paid work and family work, which, in turn, calls for a re-evaluation of the concept of 'work'.

## The watchword should be 'quality'

69. The development of mass education and vocational training at all levels — a result of enormous effort — has pointed to the need for 'quality' as a process of continuous application of effort, in order to make education and training better adapted to the constraints of international competition and business sector requirements.

70. The concept of quality may be readily evident for the world of business, but its translation into the world of education and training systems is less readily evident. Quality assurance basically means placing the client or user of a service at the centre of concern, rather than the perspectives and practices of service providers. From an economic standpoint, to ask this of education and training systems is normal enough. The problem is how to get our systems to take greater account of business sector requirements and thus offer learners the skills and qualifications companies need.

71. Put this way, the answer is relatively simple and the direction clear. Our education and training systems need to move in the direction of providing training in the occupations which are most in demand (which presupposes sound information on these occupations); to take due account of the speed at which occupations are renewed; and thus to provide transversal key skills enabling people to switch occupation; to increase the level of technological understanding; and to provide the basis for the intercultural skills required for an international working environment. Today, this demand is less fundamentally opposed to the educational tradition of

developing autonomous subjects endowed with a strong critical spirit and a capacity to call into question the structures of economic and social life. Large organisations have exactly these demands. Preparing young Europeans for a process of learning throughout life is also part of the quest for quality, which must be a concern that begins at the primary school. This presupposes arousing curiosity, a permanent desire to improve and the development of adaptability.

72. The Study Group wants to underline, at this point, that excessive diversification of specialised diplomas so that the requirements of very specific occupations can be precisely targeted is not the answer. Several countries have tried to develop vocational training at a frantic pace in order to keep up. They have thus established a range of training that is often outpaced by occupational trends themselves; sometimes training courses have been producing at maximum level when the occupation itself has disappeared. Despite a few successes, this has contributed to making these diplomas worthless, the result being that vocational channels have all lost out to general training channels.

73. Adhering to 'quality' guidelines in the education system thus makes it necessary to take account of three linked questions which imply a radical change in practices and mentalities, both within the business sector and the education system: (i) how to blend in the development of the whole person, which is the prime aim of education, with the quest for quality of human resources in the business sector sense, (ii) methods of teaching/learning and the ways in which the acquisition of cognitive and social skills can coincide, (iii) how to reduce labour market uncertainty or at least to be able to manage labour market risks. This uncertainty casts a shadow over the future and encourages the retention of more conservative perspectives.

## Push for qualifications or filter out the best deductive brains?

74. In view of international competition and the rising tide of unemployment in Europe, the Group considers, as stated in the White Paper 'Teaching and learning: towards the learning society', that wanting to develop people's potential without offering them realistic job prospects is a delusion. Our educational establishments now contain many students who do not know why they are following this or that course of study, and who are becoming increasingly worried and disenchanted as regards their future chances of getting jobs.

Just think what they are up against: either they manage to get onto highly selective courses or those which are targeted at the occupations of the future — and in this case they have a clear job prospect ahead — or else they fail to do so and say to themselves that it is better to follow their initial inclinations for a given sector and stay as long as possible within the education system and, even at the cost of having no clear job prospects, at least do something they enjoy. What makes it worse is that often they have no other option than to go for the areas which do not correspond to their vocational aspirations; there are vacancies in all apprenticeship centres for the less popular trades.

Most European countries have more or less devised 'transitions systems' between education, training and the labour market that come into operation between the end of compulsory schooling and entry to higher education. However, the fact remains that the duration of studies has substantially increased and rising university enrolments for human and social sciences seems to corroborate how widespread the behaviour described above is.

While the humanities and social sciences have a major role to play within the university and in promoting key qualities needed for life and occupations, there is a danger that too many students drift into them and do not achieve the potential of these studies. There is a need to guard the quality assurance indicators for such courses and to encourage some cross-disciplinary work with the natural and applied sciences. On the other hand, these latter subjects, as well as some applied professional disciplines, are failing to attract and retain sufficient numbers of students and also need to incorporate elements of humanist disciplines. Greater interdisciplinarity of studies would be of benefit for contemporary economic and social demands. Changing this state of affairs is a major venture, for it implies changing practices in companies, among the social partners, in educational establishments, and amongst families and young people themselves.

75. There is a huge gap here between what is generally said and what is actually done, so much so that the behaviour of our young people can be considered to be coherent. Indeed, it is our young people who have seen the reality of things, rather than believing what they have continually been told about the qualities they need to find employment. The reality remains clearly as follows. The most efficient and the most dynamic small and large enterprises in Europe (those which offer the jobs we would all like for our children), recruit on the basis of paper qualifications and the standing of the awarding institution, except in those cases where companies themselves participate in the training process of potential recruits. Yet the

standing of educational establishments is directly linked to the number of applicants they attract in relation to the numbers they accept. In certain countries selection is based on the quality of the candidates assessed on the basis of their level of academic achievement (dominant factor: ranking in relation to fellow-candidates in the same class), of their motivation and their relational skills. In others, the level of academic achievement is given pride of place. Mathematics have become a key discriminator in selection, including in several social science areas (management, economics, and even psychology) or health-related subject areas, so that performance in this subject is now a central issue (a notable exception is law).

76. While there is a plentiful supply of highly formally qualified people (and the demand for such recruits are low), these enterprises choose the applicants whom they consider to be in best possession of the social and personal skills that correspond to their organisational culture or the occupation to which they are recruiting. Should none of the applicants meet these criteria, enterprises nevertheless recruit the best (paper-) qualified and provide in-service training to make up the deficits. Everything points to the widespread use of this mechanism; this comes out in particular through the comparative salary levels or the placement of recruits in the organisation. This phenomenon manifests itself equally with respect to those who achieve higher education diplomas through social mobility, 'sandwich' training courses, and self-directed learning.

77. Alongside this demand from open and competitive companies, it should not be forgotten that there are still many jobs with a low innovation content and which do not need the skills demanded for recruitment. Even at management level, university teachers now frequently come across former students who stress the gap between what they have learned and what is expected of them on the job; they are less likely to hear former students say that they were inadequately prepared for the demands of their work. The often routine nature of the tasks they are called upon to fulfil, [1] the hierarchy of the structures which they meet in many companies, and the lack of co-operation which prevails there, — none of these features correspond to the archetype of the co-operative, learning and innovating enterprise that the Business Schools teach about. For many young people, this simply strengthens the feeling that they are better off doing 'something interesting' (literature, philosophy, sociology, history, psychology, etc. [2] in higher education, rather than preparing themselves to be overqualified for a routine job.

---

[1] This is something which is obviously even more keenly felt by manual workers. A recent survey conducted in France among industrial workers shows that 60% of them feel that they are locked into repetitive tasks.

[2] Social sciences today provide the largest single slice of higher education qualifications in Europe (25%).

This also shows that the changes needed in the education system must go hand in hand with parallel changes in the business sector. [1]

78. In reality, educational systems are therefore required to function as a hierarchical talent filter. The systems' players have fulfilled this function by 'adjusting upwards', operating on the principle that their job is to ensure the 'best minds' go as far as possible up the ladder of academic achievement in general education and for the chosen subject area. With some exceptions (in particular, Germany and Sweden), educational systems have dealt with the question of fulfilling business sector needs by

**Graph F6: Higher education students by field of study (estimate for 12 Member States), 1992/93**

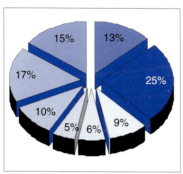

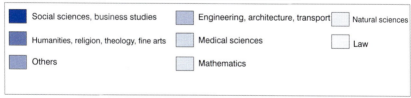

*Source:* Key data on education in the European Union, 1995 Edition.

*Data:* Eurostat.

**Belgium, France** and **Luxembourg**: Data not available.
**Austria**: Some students are included in more than one subject area.
**United Kingdom**: Law is included under Humanities, religion etc. Information and documentation is included under Other.

EXPLANATORY NOTE

*Eurostat generally distinguishes eight fields of study: Humanities, religion and theology; Social sciences (commercial and business administration, mass media); Law; Natural sciences; Mathematics and computer sciences; Medical sciences; Engineering, architecture (transport, trade, craft and industrial programmes); Others (education; agriculture; services sector; others unspecified).*

---

[1] Key Data on Education in the European Union '95, Graphic F6: Higher education students by subject of study. Estimates of European rates from twelve countries. 1992/3, Annex 2.

developing over-narrow vocational education and training tracks, which are then accorded a lower status by the education system itself (for example, less favourable all-round conditions for the teachers; counselling pupils who do less well in general education to change to vocational tracks, and so on).

79. The important point is that private and public enterprises and the social partners still accept this situation and, by their own actions, continue to confirm it. In certain countries, private and public organisations have even aggravated the situation by establishing their own training systems and thus introducing even more elitism (e.g. France). Throughout the world, everything is structured in such a way that school leads to even more school, whereas enterprises select the best products from the various tracks at the different exit levels. The fact that much education, particularly at university level, is designed to produce the tiny minority who will go on to pursue academic research in the discipline itself, inevitably means neglect by the university of the development of broader transferable skills, managerial/supervisory skills, or our own notions of ethics and citizenship explored in Chapter II. This is accentuated by the fact that the course of subsequent work careers is strongly associated with having achieved a record of academic excellence at a young age (a major exception once again being Germany[1]). A point worth stressing is that Japan, whom everyone agrees to be the inventor of collective learning processes at work, has an education system which is based to the extreme on the selection of a 'generalist' elite (selection begins very early, when children transfer from lower secondary to upper secondary education).

## A new match between the acquisition of knowledge and the development of behavioural patterns

80. The changes needed in teaching and learning methods are also affected by this situation. Teachers who practice the 'filtering function' referred to earlier work on the basis of a particular concept of personal development, one which is almost exclusively oriented towards the acquisition of a

---

[1] Over a quarter of the managing directors of the major German-origin companies came up through the apprenticeship route. A higher education qualification is nevertheless very important, but this frequently comes following a return to higher education after a first period on the employment market as a self-taught person. At the same time, it should be noted that over half of top German bosses hold doctorates, although these do not come from particular universities.

In France, Italy, Spain and the United Kingdom power is concentrated in the hands of former students of some 'grandes écoles' or universities. In France, this phenomenon has atrophied around certain grandes écoles; in the UK, over three-quarters of the top administration in the big companies attended a public school and then went on to Oxford or Cambridge; a third of the upper strata in the City, despite substantial institutional upheaval, come from Eton (John Scott, The recruitment of elites in Europe, 1995).

specific variety of cognitive knowledge, i.e., learning a subject discipline. This kind of acquisition, and learning the methods for doing so on a continuous basis, is a crucial element in fulfilling personal potential that cannot be underestimated. The rigorous discipline required to do so prompts children and adults to make a personal, inevitably solitary, effort to assimilate concepts, abstract terminology, ways of organising reasoning that uses these concepts, and to attempt applications of that reasoning. This experience is irreplaceable, particularly because it lends a sense of confidence in oneself. Moreover, it is perfectly natural that schools, in seeking quality, think they are obligated to teach all their pupils good working habits and the skills for knowledge acquisition. After all, paper qualifications attest intellectual achievement on an individual basis, and in this context the spirit of competition is by no means absent. Neither do companies conclude collective employment contracts. The way in which the 'filtering system' functions equally imposes an obligation upon schools to provide a 'fair' framework for ranking children's individual achievements in order to reflect their respective attributes and efforts. Whenever educational systems have been tempted to follow 'fashionable utopias' that seek to break with these filtering mechanisms that are founded in a form of individual competition, the experiments have failed: education has disconnected itself both from the business world and, more generally, from our societies, which do not work that way.

81. However, while maintaining these inescapable principles, major changes in teaching and learning methods are clearly necessary. In the first place, the quantity of knowledge that children must assimilate from the outset of secondary schooling is becoming impossible to manage — and becomes plainly absurd when the deductive approach is given priority. Despite substantial efforts to improve the situation, 12-year old children frequently find themselves confronted with a dozen or so subjects, each of which has its own concepts and terminology (whereas their methods of reasoning are very similar). It is therefore necessary to develop an interdisciplinary approach and to place greater emphasis on inductive and experimental approaches. Social skills then require enhancement, which implies group work methods. The problem here is to valorise the capacity to work, learn and innovate within a team, because our social organisation places the emphasis on individual competition, just as schools do.

82. However, a resolute step is needed in this direction, *inter alia* by assessing group capacity through collective examinations. This implies striking a delicate balance between these forms of accreditation and the more traditional forms, and also appropriate instruments of evaluation. This will imply substantial cultural upheaval in schools which, once again, can only

be envisaged if the business sector itself moves in the same direction. How many organisations today, which 'officially' emphasise the personal-social skills of communication and solidarity, become the scene of competition on the inside for places of responsibility? How many companies offer over-specific and incomplete visions of their tasks to the men and women who work in them? School can take a real step in this direction when the business sector offers an overall vision to their personnel and succeeds in rallying it around an organised common strategy. A major advance will have been accomplished once these skills are accredited as seriously as the others and recognised by companies and the social partners, not as 'add-ons' to a traditional general paper qualification, but as part and parcel of their overall skills.

83. The Study Group considers that it is thus necessary to develop the collective 'can-do' approach which will be useful to today's companies and those to be created tomorrow. It does seem that work, as an activity, is evolving towards a focus on problem-solving, and the problems that must be solved cross established knowledge, skills and occupational boundaries. Therefore, it is necessary to encourage both multidisciplinary problem-solving skills and the social-communicative competence required to work in problem-solving teams. By increasing the capacity to co-operate and to take action, education and training systems will take a decisive step forward for Europe. In addition, part of this 'can-do' philosophy could be translated into criterion-referenced basic academic skills which would be a powerful tool in eliminating discrimination for low-skill jobs.

84. From this point of view, vocational training must be able to act as a catalyst, for it is not subject to the constraints of the educational world. In its complementary function, vocational training can attempt to introduce these practices on a widespread basis, on the condition that individual achievements can be evaluated transparently and using criterion-referenced assessment. Innovative enterprises — among these, notably multinational companies — do want these kinds of changes, and have made some progress as far as developing and evaluating personal and social skills is concerned. They should be able to disseminate their experience to other institutions. But this clearly implies a radical change in how business co-operates with other education and training players. Developing personal and social skills has meant major investment and is an element of company competitiveness, so enterprises will only disseminate their expertise if there is clearer social recognition of their training role.

# Controlling employment market uncertainty more efficiently

85. The current functioning of the labour market, seen in overall terms, must be taken into account in the quest for quality through education and training. Occupations are changing in parallel with work systems; all predictions of both individual and collective occupational and employment features are uncertain. This problem is compounded by current labour market equilibria. What, for instance, do we tell young men and women aged 22-23 coming to the end of their university studies who know that the demand for managerial recruits in Europe will account for just over a third of the candidates eligible to apply after completing initial education and training? Clearly many young people will have to adjust their immediate expectations and accept supervisory level or other jobs initially. We should tell them to continue their lifelong learning from a work base, however meagre. This upward qualifications drift — overqualified graduates filling intermediate jobs — may or may not be a temporary feature of our labour markets, depending on their long-term growth and competitiveness. However, it is clear that this trend towards potential over-qualification shunts unemployment and low lifetime earnings towards the least qualified. The fact remains, in most if not all Member States, that the chance and duration of unemployment are inversely correlated with level of qualifications and in consequence high qualifications still mean very significantly above average lifetime earnings.

86. The strategic uncertainties in the business sector correspond with uncertainties in the world of education. Companies and their representative organisations have never been particularly good at predicting their personnel needs in terms of numbers or qualifications. With a few notable exceptions, the various efforts made since the early 1970s to predict jobs and skills have proved very difficult to convert into fully operational management tools. Nevertheless, one should look positively at the efforts that are being made to develop and co-ordinate employment and skills upgrading within and across regions. Certain urban zone, area employment pools and regions are aware of their assets and are pursuing interesting policies which aim to use and manage their skills optimally and with a view to the future. This is a new area of co-operation which should be developed, particularly in order to give it a clearer European dimension.

87. Nowadays, the growing complexity of relations between markets, technologies and products is making it much more difficult to define corporate strategies. Even in sectors which require the highest rates of research and development and hence optimum forecasting capability, short-term plan-

ning is becoming more dominant and has constraining effects. Difficulties in formulating economic strategies result in difficulties in defining human resources strategies. As a result, companies are finding it increasingly difficult to formulate medium and long-term views of their skills needs. In the current phase of heightened global competition, the dominant concern is wage costs. The current priority is therefore to seek methods and programmes which can induce companies to reinvest in human intelligence. We also need to put more effort into the prediction management of employment, qualifications and skills needs. Lastly, skills development must be recognised as an appropriate field for dialogue between the social partners and with the workforce at enterprise and sector level. The progress made in accreditation arrangements should undoubtedly accompany new arrangements for dialogue and recognition of skills obtained in the collective systems and, why not, in the context of the wage contract, too.

88. The dominance of short-term planning horizons is also reflected in companies' reluctance to consider new ways of organising work and skills. Yet these would enable us to derive more benefit from the cognitive competencies with which the labour market has been provided by our countries' investments in education and training to date. The reluctance to take this into account means that companies seriously underestimate both individuals' capacity to adapt and the extent to which their skills are transferable. A common result is that companies express demands for more training effort, when in fact they need to change their organisational structures.

89. So what might have been nothing more than a problem of company economics thus turns into a general problem in that firms appeal to society as a whole to meet their falsely perceived training needs. 'Think globally, act locally' remains a consultant's slogan. More particularly, companies may be failing to mobilise the creative abilities of their staff. This then turns into an inflated demand for more company-external training in order to lend impulse to innovation. These deficiencies should not conceal the fact that the development of continuing training and the establishment of training plans in companies are essential. Companies have not responded sufficiently to the scale of continuing training needs and demands; and there are marked inequalities of provision between categories of enterprise. We should add that expenditure on continuing training remains too dependent on the economic conjuncture. Considerable progress needs to be made so that such expenditure is treated as real company investment.

90. Impermeable company hierarchies — whether vertical or horizontal — are a significant obstacle to the full utilisation of educational investment. If organisational hierarchies were to be opened up, this might reduce some of the demand for public and privately funded education and training. Such organisational reforms become all the more necessary insofar as changes in work situations themselves modify the conditions for continuing skills acquisition in enterprises. Those companies that are aware of these issues are exploring new ways of expanding learning opportunities and developing internal knowledge communications networks. These trends are to be encouraged and disseminated throughout the business world, in particular to resolve the problems in access to training in SMEs.

91. Two consequences arise. Firstly, more emphasis will be placed on individual responsibility for making education and training choices. People need to be prepared for living in a rapidly moving and unpredictable world. With specific exceptions, it is an illusion to suppose that our education and training systems can definitively position young people on a particular occupational or career track. Secondly, organic links between the labour market and the education system must be developed, with continuous co-operation between all players (especially between schools, companies and local authorities). Working closely together is the key to simultaneous change in both educational and business systems; this will also provide everyone involved with the information needed to decide how to acquire and update their knowledge and skills on a lifelong basis. And, finally, close co-operation will enable us to identify and update those new occupational profiles that will replace the old 'trades'. Such profiles need to put much greater emphasis on core/key transferable skills; they also need to be designed in 'non-gendered' ways, so that such new occupational profiles appeal to and are accessible to both women and men in equal measure.

## Coming out on top by creating a virtuous circle of innovation

92. The quest for quality will come into its own if it is pursued in a context of creativity and innovation. Innovation creates the basis for new activities and rising European productivity. From the company's point of view this means that human resources must develop new qualities. The new workforce must be oriented towards problem-solving, prepared to learn and relearn on a continuous basis, and integrated into work environments that permanently seek new technical solutions and processes.

93. By and large, to generate new ideas means making suggestions for change, which implies a substantial dose of creativity on the part of those concerned; the role of research is crucial in this context. The organisation which will be best at generating ideas will be the one which will have best used all its human resources. Everyone's participation is required — not only for ethical or social reasons, but in order to enhance corporate effectiveness. More creativity is generated when a substantial number of persons are involved in the process. While everyone acknowledges that the management of creativity poses difficulties, it is equally clear that creativity develops when the working climate, the tools and the motivation are positive.

94. Creativity is the overall process which begins an intellectual speculation that spurs the imagination and concludes when an innovation is implemented. Everyone knows that change generates problems. These are always problems linked to people's respective places in the social environment. Each one of these problems is managed by a person whose role is to modify the situation in line with the direction chosen. To solve the problem, it is essential for that person to be able to identify the exact state of play at any given time. Management of the implementation of innovation is part of the general question of **problem-solving.**

95. This highlights a paradox. Problem-solving methods are so important in practice, but they are seldom taught at school. They are generally hidden within a 'standard approach' to formal problem-solving for specific subject disciplines. Children at school learn to solve mathematics problems (often algebra or trigonometry, more rarely pure mathematics), physics problems, and so on. The methods themselves are not usually made explicit. Via some mysterious process, the pupil is expected to acquire a genuine capacity to solve problems in that subject. Even the best pupils cannot manage this. Specific and under-explicated problem-solving approaches for specific subjects should be replaced with a general approach to problem-solving.

96. Problem-solving processes have been developed within each culture as an intrinsic part of their approach to life. Different cultures in different environments have used different approaches. The Cartesian approach to problem-solving dominates Western culture. This approach divides a problem into parts, solves the issues relating to each part, and puts the partial solutions together in order to obtain 'the solution' to the overall problem. The Cartesian approach is well suited to engineering problems, for example, which have a 'composite' structure that can be broken down into constituent elements. Oriental problem-solving cultures dislike sepa-

rating wholes into parts: the whole is more than the sum of its parts, and is thus not additive. Therefore, the whole must be taken as it is, because the features of its behaviour as a phenomenon cannot be appreciated or derived from the elements that make up the whole. This kind of approach does not yield the same results as the Cartesian method. It is better suited, for example, to social problems; it is undoubtedly less well suited to others. Be that as it may, multinational companies have made the teaching of problem-solving one of the pillars of their consolidation and renewal strategy.

97. The other implication of this trend is that problem-solving encourages learning and that the development of learning enhances a central component of every company, i.e. its knowledge base. In modern innovatory organisations, maintaining a competitive edge is the key to survival. Competitivity hinges on the possession, management and replenishment of this knowledge base.

98. To enter into the modern world and be capable of innovating, organisations must therefore establish a virtuous circle which is decisive for their survival. Creativity will make it possible to start a process of innovation. The implementation of this process of innovation will engender problems. The solution of these problems will emerge from the learning of new skills. These skills will enter into the organisation's knowledge base. And it is the accretion of this knowledge base which will enhance company competitiveness.

99. In the context of education and training these trends have two consequences: (i) if we want to position ourselves well in the learning society of the future, our education and training systems must produce creative persons with a greater capability for problem-solving; (ii) if these persons are to acquire new skills, education and training establishments themselves need to become organisations which give priority to quality and innovation.

## The way forward for Europe

100. The Study Group considers that Europe must make full use of its assets to renew education and training in order to improve the competitiveness of European human capital. This perspective is limited to the economic aspects of education and training, but there are considerable social and human consequences, particularly in the current situation. In order to make progress in terms of quality and innovation, Europe must help to

make progress on: (i) the relationship between general education, which provides basic knowledge and develops general culture, and vocational training, which develops aptitudes and behaviours; (ii) the definition and comparability of skills acquired, (iii) the definition and acquisition of new 'occupational profiles'.

In the framework of its strategy to promote employment, Europe is increasingly placing the emphasis on factors linked to competencies and their development throughout individuals' lives. The Study Group supports this strategy and, within that, the idea of Community level action that promotes lifelong learning itself, diverse modes of access to continuing education and training, and co-operation between all actors involved in order to make these aims a reality.

## The relationship between general education and vocational training

101. The relationship between general education and vocational training prompts two key questions. Firstly, should we continue to distinguish between the two? This is a question of principle. Secondly, what should the relationships be between the players involved in education and training (including the education and training systems, the business sector, the State, regional and local authorities, the social partners)? This is a question of organisation.

102. Rapid occupational changes and the need to ensure mastery of basic knowledge necessarily lead, in the Study Group's view, to the adoption of a general principle: **general education must provide preparation for a vocational skill, and vocational training must continue to develop the basic competencies provided by general education**. The application of this principle leads to the following consequences:

- in compulsory schooling, basic competencies should be acquired in the general education system;

- teaching and learning methods should only use abstract deduction in those few areas where it seems essential. A substantial effort should be made in other areas to develop experimentation and to use methods that foster learning to 'sense' the nature of problems and problem-solving. Europe should take steps to identify and disseminate best practice and the results achieved;

78

- teaching people to work as part of a group (*inter alia* by using information technologies) demands considerable effort. This also demands progress to identify the skills acquired through group work, to accredit group work in the same way as individual work, and to introduce and gain acceptance for the unambiguous evaluation of individual behavioural skills, in particular communication skills, leadership and problem-solving.6 Ultimately, these assessments of behavioural patterns must become as 'solid' as traditional assessments. European research funds should make resources available for these tasks;

- cross-curricular approaches should be developed in upper primary and at secondary school in order to show the methodological similarities between different subject areas to reduce passive forms of pupil learning, and to allow room for group projects and the acquisition of behavioural aptitudes.

103. Two approaches dominate the **organisation** of the relationships between general education and initial vocational training. The first is the 'dual system', in which education and training take place both at school and in the workplace. In dual systems, companies deliver the majority of vocational training, whereas schools are wholly responsible for general education. In the second kind of system, both general and vocational education and training takes place in schools and colleges, which then convince the business sector to co-operate.[1] A third system, in which all vocational training takes place at the workplace, is less widespread (the most developed example of this system is in the United Kingdom).[2]

Germany and, to a lesser extent, Luxembourg, the Netherlands, Belgium, Denmark and Sweden have adopted dual systems. Youth unemployment rates in these countries are lower, and have developed differently over time, than elsewhere in Europe. Whilst this indicates advantages of the dual system, this does not imply that the rest of Europe should adopt

---

[1] This is unavoidable in view of the importance currently attached to attitudes and behavioural patterns and does not only raise technical questions. It also raises fundamental ethical questions which must be an integral part of the research programme. Evaluating behavioural aptitudes should not be used as a pretext for carrying out personal assessment (in the traditional Anglo-Saxon sense of 'character'). This would lead to a kind of 'personality bodystyling'! But it is necessary to make progress in the field of education for social skills.

[2] It should be noted here that across the European Union, there are higher numbers of young people registered in upper level vocational secondary education than in upper level general secondary education; this is the case for eleven Member States (Key Data on Education in the European Union '95, Graph E3, percentage of pupils in second cycle general and vocational secondary education (CITE 3), academic year 1992/3, annex 3).

## Graph E3: Percentages of pupils in general and vocational upper secondary education (ISCED 3), 1992/93

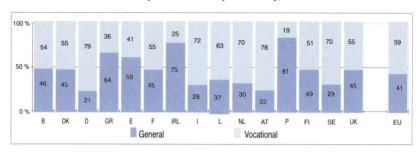

*Source:* Key data on education in the European Union, 1995 Edition.

*Data:* Eurostat.

**Belgium**: This is an estimate.
**Luxembourg**: Data provided by the Ministry of Education.
**United Kingdom (E/W and NI)**: There is no separate upper secondary vocational education. This represents post-compulsory vocational education.

**In the European Union as a whole, there are more pupils in vocational than in general upper secondary education. This is the case in 11 Member States.**

This trend is particularly marked in Germany, Italy, the Netherlands, Austria and Sweden. Conversely, there are more pupils in general education in Greece, Spain, Ireland and Portugal.

---
EXPLANATORY NOTE
---

*Upper secondary education corresponds to ISCED level 3. In Graph E3, the distribution of pupils between the two types of education is based on the total numbers of pupils in education. From the data available, it is not possible to take into account students undertaking vocational training within businesses.*

---

the dual system as such. Nevertheless, the success of the dual system shows that:

- whenever possible, the business sector should be significantly involved in vocational training both because this is more effective — in that this ensures modern techniques and working practices are learnt — and because the business sector is more likely to recognise people who have received their vocational training by this route;

- a training and learning culture needs to be stimulated at company level:

  * employees must be able to train continually, their efforts must be rewarded, and their practical experience in enterprises should be valorised,

  * the company's aims in terms of development of knowledge and qualifications of the workforce should be clearly stated,

* company employees involved in training (in particular, mentors) should have greater support and recognition within the company;

• schools and teachers should concentrate on providing good-quality general education; this is their job. They have everything to gain, because they could give priority to the acquisition of knowledge and to pupils' personal development. This means that school acknowledges that one way or another the company intervenes within its walls to provide vocational training or at least to get involved in it;

• the business sector and educational establishments should co-operate closely, in conjunction with the social partners, so that each general education track can be designed within a vocational perspective, and so that each vocational training track can provide solid elements of general education. In an ideal system of such co-operation, **teachers would be responsible for general education subjects in general education tracks in schools and for general education subjects within vocational training tracks organised by the business sector. Company and other vocational trainers would be responsible for the vocational elements of general education tracks at school and for vocational training offered within the company**. This co-operation could take a number of forms; all need to be developed:

  * organisation of new types of apprenticeship and work experience placements of pupils and students,

  * exchange of experience between mentors and teachers,

  * joint development (companies-students) of curriculum materials and sharing of high-cost teaching resources, i.e. use of education equipment and use of school and university buildings for initial and continuing training,

  * more open participation by vocational training tutors and general education teachers on each other's examination boards;

• work experience and in-company placements are decisive factors for recruitment. Such practices must allow for subsequent return to general education at a higher level.

## Graph A7: Youth unemployment rates by country, 1983-93

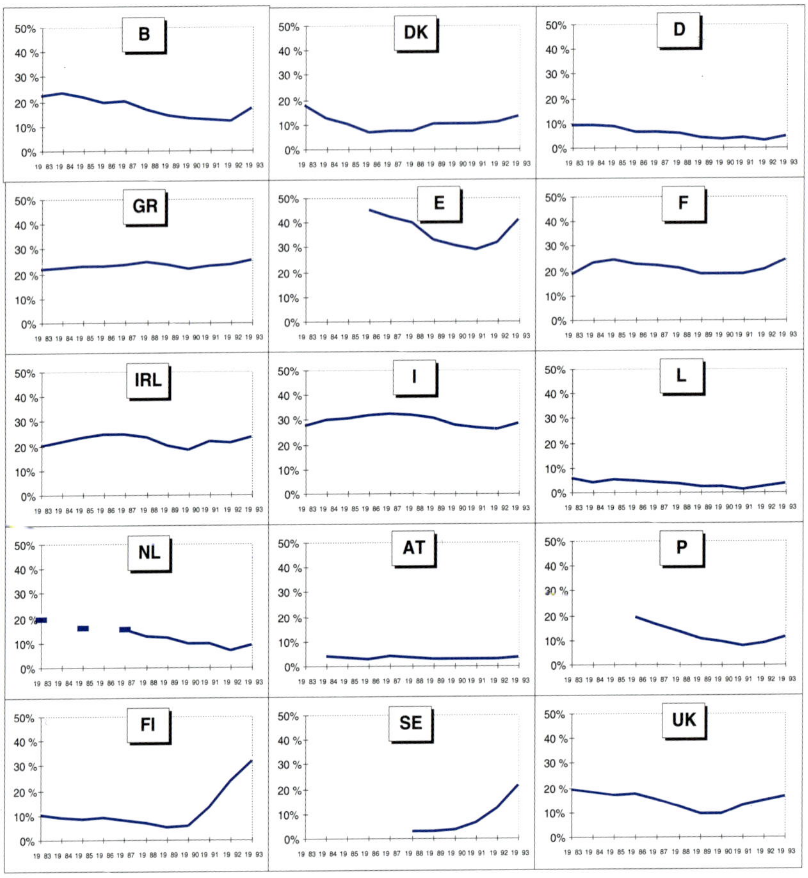

Source: Key data on education in the European Union, 1995 Edition.

Data: Eurostat, Labour force survey.

**Austria, Finland** and **Sweden**: Data provided by the national statistical offices.

> EXPLANATORY NOTE
>
> *The unemployment rates have been harmonized for the 12 Member States in 1983. Differences are only likely to occur concerning the data for the three new Member States. In 1992 however, there was a change in the definition of unemployment which can cause a slight break in the time series.*

104. All this means that the permeability between the education world and the business sector must be increased. Company trainers must be allowed to take part in general education for vocational areas, and teachers should be allowed to take part in vocational training for general subject areas. This implies an intensive training drive for vocational trainers and schoolteachers, one in which Europe could become involved. This will

also imply establishing a framework of co-operation between the social partners, the State and the local authorities for general education and vocational training alike. Once again, the German Chambers of Commerce and Chambers of Craft Trades and the British Training and Enterprise Councils (TECs) and education/business partnerships could be useful from this point of view. Lastly, European multinationals have identified social and behavioural skills, and have learnt how to develop and validate these. This expertise should be turned to good account in education and training systems. This presupposes that these activities are recorded and that provision is made for their widespread introduction. European-level action should be envisaged for these tasks.

## The definition and comparability of skills acquired

105.  Strengthening the comparability of skills acquired in European education and training systems is essential for three reasons: (i) the mobility of people in Europe, (ii) the evaluation of teaching and learning systems, (iii) self-tuition and lifelong learning.

106.  Today, the EU is a single market; tomorrow, it will become a monetary Union. The circulation of goods was possible because a standard measure existed (the ECU and the dollar) for relative product prices. The movement of people will gather pace once a system for evaluating the skills they acquire in initial or continuing general/vocational education and training. The slow progress made in the mutual recognition of qualifications is a perfect illustration of how difficult it is to increase intra-European mobility of people without a yardstick, even an approximate one, for measuring the content on which these skills are based. It is today anachronistic not to move ahead more swiftly in this direction.

107.  The second reason is the lack of evaluation of what young people or adults who follow education and training courses know (in terms of knowledge, know-how and attitudes). Institutional evaluation is not the only way to move ahead, because this naturally promotes elitism and ultimately offers no true reflection of the skills levels of the people involved. It is more important to be able to evaluate what learners know when they leave a given training course. This is an urgent requirement in vocational training. A number of countries (Belgium, Denmark, France, Ireland, Portugal, Greece) have instituted processes for accrediting training centres. The UK has attempted an innovatory and in principle fully appropriate national system of competence-based criterion-referenced vocational qualifications designed by business-led teams, in which

trainees are assessed on what they can actually do in the workplace environment. It is clearly through the Europe-wide introduction of such systems that: (i) the training market will become more transparent, (ii) we will have a 'standard' which will boost European mobility for non-regulated occupations. At the same time, it is important to ensure that enterprises are served with the flexible qualifications profiles and structures that they need. If taken too far, grids of qualification equivalencies run the risk of slipping into a purely administrative logic which rigidly specifies that *'this* qualification gives access to *that* kind of job'.

108. In this context, the Study Group entered into the current debate on the respective potentials offered by the concepts of competence/skill and qualification.

In the first approach to this issue, the concept of qualification is understood as a 'social object' that articulates different forms of knowledge in an education and training context that is well-defined and precisely operationalised. In this approach, the sole guarantee for solid educational provision is that offered through an institutionalised system which furnishes recognised diplomas anchored in a qualifications grid negotiated between the social partners. Two members of the Group took the firm view that education provision must remain solely within this mode.

The second approach considers that the coming of the Information Society, the effects of globalisation, the weakening links between the possession of particular formal qualifications and secure job prospects, and the necessity for continuous re-training all require a reformulation of the concept of competence/skill to include an *'attribut privé'* which could very well be certified independently of the institution or context in which that competency has been acquired. This approach conforms to that proposed in the White Paper *Teaching and learning: towards the learning society,* which puts forward the idea of providing complementary modes of certification to that of the formally-acquired diploma. These might address themselves to partial or modular competencies, which could be acquired in a 'free' manner (that is, with or without recourse to the formal system) and which can be pursued within the framework of lifelong learning. To give an example of what is meant here, one might say that tennis players' individual competence levels cannot solely be attributed to the quality of the sports training programmes they have followed. They are a function of personal aptitudes that are realised in open competition. Moreover, their progress depends on continuously re-launched efforts and not on the basis of a certificate awarded at a particular age by their sports training centre which attests their attainment of a given level. This necessarily limited 'non-institutionalised' concept of competence corresponds to that held by this second approach to the issue of competence/skill in contrast with qualification.

The broad majority of Study Group members support the necessity to develop the kind of system described in this second approach, which returns a measure of initiative to the responsibility of the individual, in enabling each person — no matter where or when — to try as often as she or he wishes to secure accreditation for partial competencies, howsoever these have been acquired (whether through the formal education and training system, through self-directed learning with the aid of IT, or through a range of informal means such as *universités populaires* or knowledge exchange networks). The limiting condition for the development of such a complementary system, however, is that it does not aspire to replace institutionalised accreditation systems and that it is not conceived as a 'diluted knowledge' system. This means that such a complementary system should not focus on interdisciplinary knowledge where there have been debates over schools of thought (history, philosophy, sociology, etc.). The system should be dynamic in nature and considered as complementary to the formal accreditation system. Moreover, it is clear to the Study Group members that during the period of compulsory schooling it is difficult to break up the educational process into modules and this implies a strong horizontality of learning that is only compatible with the institutional approach first described above.

109. In sum, and in following up the Commission's White Paper *Teaching and learning: towards the learning society*, the above points imply:

- defining skills reference charts;

- introducing systems for accrediting skills;

- making these accreditation systems widely and continuously available;

- keeping a simple ongoing check of individual skills acquisition progress;

- developing recognition of vocational qualifications with the use of examination procedures that involve the social partners;

- the modularisation of education and training courses throughout Europe and at least in higher education. This presupposes that all universities switch to a semester system;

- speeding up the process for modular recognition between similar courses in European universities.

110. In order to promote the development of these ideas and practices, the following features are proposed as a checklist for action. Together, they could be seen to provide the basis for an Internet facility called 'European what do you know?':

- **Target:** all the people of the European Union.

- **Content:** certain tests of different levels for technical subjects and skills (maths, written language, spreadsheet accounting, modern languages, etc., but obviously not including philosophy, history, sociology, etc.) directly accessible via a PC. Test results are provided in real time and use software that corrects answers automatically.

- **Method:** required content is defined through joint work by national assessment/accreditation agencies and/or by dissemination of best practice throughout Europe.

- **Implementation:** further development and dissemination of experiments undertaken by the EU under Objective 1 of the White Paper *Teaching and learning: towards the learning society*.


## The new occupational profiles

111. Our industrial systems are a good example of the laws of evolution. Over time, these systems have become more complex and specialised, just as living organisms have done. Specialisation has led to the emergence of an increasing variety of occupations. Complexity has been managed by co-ordination processes in which information technologies have played a central role.

112. Education and training systems should not try to target all of these occupations[1] This is not the way forward, because occupational contents change rapidly. It is better to look at what certain groups of occupations share, at the system that co-ordinates these groups, and at key transversal skills.

113. The Group considers that, without in any manner envisaging the establishment of uniform and static systems of reglementation, Europe could help:

   • for the major industrial and service sectors, to identify the new types of company that will characterise the European economy in the next 10 years;

   • to define a limited list of generic basic occupations which do not necessarily conform to standard industrial classifications;

   • to develop occupational classification systems by bringing those that are currently used closer together;

   • to specify the main 'occupational profiles' needed in the future,

   • to define for these occupational profiles those skills that should be developed in initial vocational training and those that could be developed across active working life.

114. In order to work towards defining 'European occupational profiles', it is proposed to establish a limited number of occupational committees (for the main sectors) at the European level, which meet regularly and whose task is to:

   (i)   study occupational classifications and suggest changes to bring them closer together and reduce their number;

   (ii)  identify generic occupations and occupational profiles needed;

   (iii) offer opinions on the skills thus needed.

---

[1] Cf. Key Data on Education in the European Union '95, Graph A7: unemployment rates among young people by country between 1983 and 1993, annex 4.
It should be noted, however, that comparisons between unemployment rates for 25-34-year olds do not favour Germany to the same extent. This suggests that after a period of apprenticeship in which young people are paid one-third of the minimum salary the problem is worse than elsewhere. Another explanation for the particularly low youth unemployment rate in Germany is the moral commitment to the plight of young people by the German community, the business sector and the social partners. The business sector, in particular, feels it has to maintain specific obligations vis-à-vis young people.

These networks should not have any harmonising purpose. On the contrary, they should function on principles of co-operation, in bringing together the social partners and representatives of national education and training systems at the European level. Committees of this type already exist in all countries in one form or another. Their working principle should be to promote synergy in the work of existing structures and committees in the Member States and in the initiatives developed through Community programmes. Their role would be propositional and consultative.

# IV. Maintaining social cohesion through education and training

## The need for social cohesion

115. Youth is not a biological reality that recurs with each generation; youth is a differentiated social reality, a reality that changes across historical time and cultural space. Some will consider it inappropriate to consider how schooling and training should fulfil their tasks of social integration and upward mobility at a time when unemployment is the main concern. There would be no urgency were it not for the general atmosphere of competition in which, as everybody knows, winners and losers are chosen and increases the gap between the two. Why be concerned with each person, with equal opportunities and with modifying structures, when we are faced with the massive phenomenon of unemployment? Should we not, instead, encourage the winners and compensate the losers with the minimum required in order to preserve social (and financial) balance?

116. The Study Group's analysis is that this would be a grave error. To progress, Europe needs to mobilise all its human potential: both young people and adults seeking to improve themselves. The current situation should in fact help us to design and share a new plan, to define its rules and to implement the plan. This is how the immigrants to New England developed the 'American dream'. How did they do it? By creating new democratic processes but also, and perhaps above all, by developing a widely shared concept of social cohesion. This gave them the necessary confidence to progress.

117. If Europe takes on this dimension, we will be able to resolve the current difficulties and restore confidence. Social cohesion may be

obtained in two ways: (i) with strong involvement by central and local public agencies who are responsible for upholding social justice as socially formulated through the democratic electoral process; this is, in general, the situation in Europe; (ii) through the collective expression of individual social conscience, which agrees on a common concept of achievement and, therefore, of failure. The 'American dream' is a good example of this second case. American society largely agrees on the legitimacy of success ('self-achievement') and has developed an awareness of 'benefit to the community' in the mind of each of its members. This is the basis for maintaining social cohesion. Considerable objective disparities in social positions have perhaps been tolerated because the 'losers' subscribe to the American dream and internalise their position as a personal failure. This is why they are less inclined to make demands on the State.

118. The situation is very different in Europe, because the social contract linking the peoples of the European nations involves the State and the public authorities. It is they who must guarantee social cohesion in most European countries, together with equal opportunities and social protection. This system has made possible great advances in education in the course of this century. It has extended universal education from primary to secondary, opened up higher education and made vocational training generally available. There is no question that this exceptional educational effort has improved the quality of human resources and encouraged social integration and mobility. This is an inalienable achievement by the peoples of Europe. Clearly, Europe should continue along this path and take care not to sacrifice the idea of developing the talents and qualifications of the entire population for the sake of short-term needs. There will be no long-term support for the new technological and market model if it is regarded as socially unjust.

119. This question has become acute with the appearance of a significant minority which becomes excluded, alienated, anti-social or apathetic: an underclass. It would be a tragic mistake for the European Union to neglect this phenomenon in favour of a frantic search for more effective economic and technological paths for the future. This search is necessary, but within a framework that consolidates existing social experience and achievements as a starting point for the simultaneous introduction of new processes of social integration.

# Consolidating existing experience and achievements

## Strengthening democratisation

120. In Europe, education and training have always had two aims. Firstly, education should be democratic, i.e. easily accessible (as inexpensive as possible, if not free) to as many people as possible. Secondly — but as a less generally shared aim — education should provide 'equal opportunities'. This means that education and training systems are open to the full development of individual potential, regardless of social origin. Educational participation rates across the whole system and to the very highest levels are used as a measure for success in achieving the first aim. The relationship between social or occupational origin and formal educational achievement measures progress towards the second aim. Whenever children from relatively disadvantaged environments or sectors of society succeed in proportion to their numbers within society, the school has succeeded in combatting social reproduction and offers opportunities for social mobility which no other social institution can provide. Education thus acts as a 'social elevator' system, which is in itself a powerful element for social cohesion.

121. All European countries have affirmed these principles, which are at the heart of the contract that exists between our societies and their education and training systems. These principles legitimate both the formation of elites and makes the corresponding existence of less advantageous social positions acceptable. A serious and permanent dysfunction at this level would without doubt be a significant obstacle to European development, including its economic development.

122. The implementation of these principles has differed according to the nature and extent of the State and local authorities, but the basic idea remains the same. In terms of the democratisation of education and training, the results are remarkable. In Sweden, over 80% of those aged 20 have a higher secondary education certificate. In eight other countries, the percentage is greater than 70% (Belgium, Denmark, Greece, France, Germany, Ireland, Netherlands, Austria and Finland). Portugal is the country with the lowest percentage (36%).[1] Secondary education does not produce discrimination to the disadvantage of girls: more girls than boys obtain a secondary leaving certificate in seven Member States

---

[1] Key Data on Education in the European Union '95, Graph E20: percentage of 20 year olds holding an upper secondary level educational diploma, 1993, annex 5.

(Denmark, Spain, France, Ireland, Italy, Portugal and Finland). [1] In almost all countries, girls are more likely than boys to hold a higher secondary certificate, but girls are much more heavily concentrated in general upper secondary education, while there are far fewer girls in vocational education. [2] On average, 15% of young people in the Union (10.7 million students registered on courses in 1992/3) are now in higher education; participation rates have risen rapidly in the 1980s. In the last 15 years, the number of students in higher education in the whole of the European Union has almost doubled. [3] Similar. efforts have been made in the field of vocational training, where on average more than 60% of today's over 25s have received vocational training, although there are still very significant disparities (over 60% in Germany, Denmark, Sweden, Finland and the Netherlands, but only 15% in Portugal). [4] The Study Group takes the view that these efforts must be continued, particularly by those countries which have not reached these levels. No form of rationing should be considered; this should also apply to access to higher education.

It is in this spirit that the Study Group affirms that nothing would be worse at present than to reduce the financial resources made available to education and training. The Group considers that Europe must promote the idea that expenditure on education — which today, on average, represents 6% of GNP — should reach, in the next ten years, on average, 8%, i.e. the average figure for the United States is 7%, for Finland it is 7.9% and Japan reaches only 4.8%. Concerning the expenditure on training, the Group thinks that it should rise to one-third, on average, in the next ten years.

123. The progress made in democratising education and training has not been matched by similar progress towards achieving real equality of opportunity. The links between social origin and formal educational success at school and university have not weakened in the last 30 years. More seriously, there is nowadays a high degree of wastage of potential, which is reflected in high failure/drop-out rates and high levels of pupil

---

[1] Key Data on Education in the European Union '95, Graph E21: percentage of girls holding upper secondary level educational diplomas, 1991/2, annex 6.

[2] Key Data on Education in the European Union '95, Graph E22: number of girls per hundred boys amongst holders of upper secondary level general educational diplomas, 1991/2; Graph E23, number of girls per hundred boys amongst holders of upper secondary level vocational educational diplomas, 1991/2, annex 7.

[3] Key Data on Education in the European Union '95, Graph F1: rates of increase in the numbers of students in higher education (CITE 5,6,7) from 1975 to 1990.

[4] Employment Observatory, Tableau de bord, European Commission, p.19.

## Graph E20: Percentages of 20-year-olds holding a certificate of upper secondary education, 1993

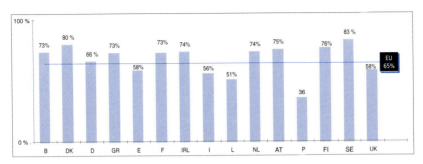

Source: Key data on education in the European Union, 1995 Edition.

Data: Eurostat labour force survey, 1993.

**Denmark**: Completed introductory year of vocational education and training included. If this is excluded, 53% of 20-year-olds hold a certificate of upper secondary education.
**Austria, Finland** and **Sweden**: The data are taken from national studies and were provided by the statistical offices given in the annex. They are not taken into account in calculating the European average.

```
┌─────────────────── EXPLANATORY NOTE ───────────────────┐
│ The Eurostat labour force survey provides statistical information with regard to employment and │
│ unemployment in the European Union. The data derive from large-scale sample surveys, which are │
│ carried out annually by the statistical offices of the Member States. The methods of data collection are │
│ devised to obtain statistical information which is optimally comparable both between countries and │
│ across years. │
└─────────────────────────────────────────────────────────┘
```

## Graph E21: Percentages of girls obtaining an upper secondary education qualification, 1991/92

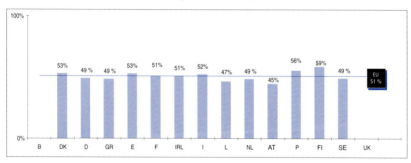

Source: Key data on education in the European Union, 1995 Edition.

Data: Eurostat.

**Belgium** and **United Kingdom**: Data not available.
**Denmark, Ireland** and **Sweden**: Data are for 1992/93.
**Luxembourg**: Data provided by the Ministry of Education.

```
┌─────────────────── EXPLANATORY NOTE ───────────────────┐
│ The breakdown between girls and boys is based on the total numbers obtaining the qualification, and │
│ not on the total population of this age. │
└─────────────────────────────────────────────────────────┘
```

93

## Graph E22: Numbers of girls (per 100 boys) obtaining general upper secondary school leaving certificates, 1991/92

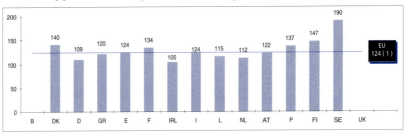

(1) European average (13 countries).

*Source:* Key data on education in the European Union, 1995 Edition.

*Data:* Eurostat.

## Graph E23: Numbers of girls (per 100 boys) obtaining vocational upper secondary school leaving certificates, 1991/92

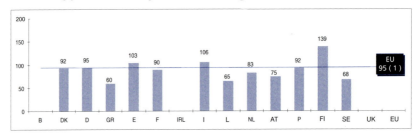

(1) European average (12 countries).

*Source:* Key data on education in the European Union, 1995 Edition.

*Data:* Eurostat.

**Belgium** and **United Kingdom**: Data not available.
**Denmark, Ireland** and **Sweden**: Data are for 1992/93.
**Luxembourg**: Data provided by the Ministry of Education.

---

EXPLANATORY NOTE

*The number of girls per 100 boys is obtained by dividing the total number of girls by the total number of boys and multiplying the result by 100.*

---

alienation. The results of a new European study shows that about 10-12% of young people do not complete compulsory schooling and therefore do not attain the basic level of education required for future Europeans.[1] In other words, schools and society in Europe are seriously out of step, which will ultimately produce social exclusion. The long-term impact of this alienation has extremely damaging effects on personal morale, attitudes, self-image and the motivation to keep on trying to succeed. Society loses too: those affected by educational failure experience a personal crisis,

---

[1] Cf. Eurydice: The struggle against school failure — a challenge for the construction of Europe, 1994.

which is reflected in the high social, health and security costs of the asocial conduct that may result. This is becoming increasingly common in countries with high immigration rates, and it must be stemmed because, in the learning society, these young people will have no opportunities, particularly since the path of self-education will be closed to them.

## Towards greater flexibility and adaptability

124. Today, this situation is a determined challenge to education and training and deserves to be examined at length. The Study Group considers that our education and training systems will only be able to take this phenomenon into account if they show greater flexibility and adaptability, for instance in their concept of the democratisation of education. What is at stake? The predominant democratic idea throughout the world of education (though less so in the world of training) is that all children, regardless of their inherent abilities, family or social circumstances, have a right to universal knowledge through education. With a number of exceptions, including special education relating to specific disabilities, this is the dominant concept in Europe, which has if anything been strengthened in recent years.[1]

125. In practice, in numerous European countries, this democratic principle has generally led to more integrated schooling, whether in the form of non-selective schools (such as comprehensive schools) or in the form of the postponement of subject specialisation or of 'tracking' until later stages of schooling, variations along these lines notwithstanding. In effect, three kinds of primary-to-secondary orientation and transfer systems exist in Europe. According to the country concerned, there may be (i) a single, non-selective system of institutional provision and teaching groups (Denmark and northern European countries); (ii) a non-selective system but institutionally separated into primary and secondary establishments (in the UK, France and southern Europe); (iii) different tracks within or between establishments from the beginning of secondary schooling (in Germany, Austria, Belgium, The Netherlands and Ireland).[2] Whilst taking into account an 'authoritarian' selection system in certain countries, children from all social backgrounds and circumstances find themselves in educational processes that aim to provide a good basic grounding in the major disciplines. The reference level 'good' is, in general, constantly rising, owing to developments in knowledge and

---

[1] Cf. J-M. Leclerc: L'enseignement secondaire obligatoire en Europe/Compulsory secondary education in Europe, OECD, 1993.

[2] Cf. European Map of directions taken at the end of primary schooling, annex 8.

in technology. We are witnessing not only an increase in the amount that children must learn but also a trend towards increasing abstraction (a phenomenon which has been pointed out earlier), which is also a strategy for managing this accumulation of new knowledge. These trends are particularly noticeable in lower secondary education, but are also present in upper secondary education, where there has been a multiplication of general education tracks throughout Europe. In higher education, the logic of subject disciplines has been reinforced together with a trend towards designing education from the top down, beginning with doctorate programmes. Meanwhile, university research has become more like a specialised industry: scientific journals have multiplied in recent years; staff recruitment and promotion is more dependent on 'performance indicators' (for example, the number of citations in the International Science Citation Index); the numbers of national and international conferences have risen dramatically; and so on. Naturally, this has created a pressure to train young researchers, but there are

## Organisation of Systems of Lower Secondary Education or in the last years of the single structure

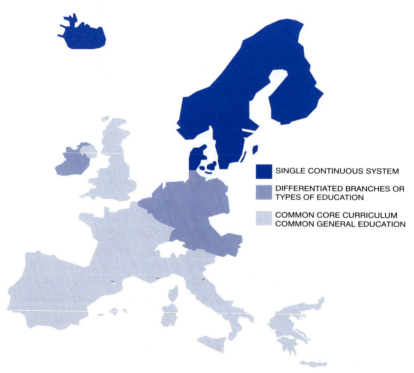

SINGLE CONTINUOUS SYSTEM

DIFFERENTIATED BRANCHES OR TYPES OF EDUCATION

COMMON CORE CURRICULUM COMMON GENERAL EDUCATION

*Source:* Pre-school and primary education in the European Union (supplement), Eurydice, February 1996.

insufficient resources to recruit them afterwards, which has resulted in significantly higher unemployment rates among the most highly-qualified university graduates (and most particularly amongst very highly-qualified women pursuing careers in research).

126. The democratisation of education is an aim that attracts fervent, convinced and disinterested support. In some countries, commitment to this aim has even been responsible for the structural patternings and policy positions taken by the teaching unions. In general, primary and lower secondary teachers working at schools in working-class areas have always shown reticence in the face of a prestigious but intimidating culture. They prefer educational systems which are more specific, closer to everyday concerns and more differentiated in order to take account of children's backgrounds and circumstances. Secondary school teachers' unions in certain countries, however, traditionally favour the idea of a single schooling system, convinced that true democracy lay in offering excellence to all. Given the importance of this question, it has been at the centre of many political debates which have only crystallised opposition and reinforced dogmatism.

127. Today, it is clear that any *a priori* aspects of these questions must be firmly set aside. Children's backgrounds and circumstances are very different; this demands that education and training systems must accept an active differentiation that aims to 'repair' the effects of these differences. Education and training systems do not actively differentiate explicitly. In certain cases, they refuse to do so in the name of the principle of democratisation. Yet education and training systems **do** differentiate implicitly either as a result of user behaviour or of the specific conditions under which they operate.

128. Today, the middle classes are leaving the inner city areas and districts with a high concentration of immigrants, because they consider they have no guarantee of a good quality education for their children. Some educational establishments become *de facto* ghettos, and this situation has an immediate and still further damaging effect on the urban environment. In contrast, the upper layers of society use all means available, including the choice of housing close to a prestigious school, in order that their children may benefit from high-quality education. Additionally, in countries where selection in general education begins at an early age, parents able to do so pay for supplementary private education on a large scale. The most significant case is Japan, where there has been considerable development in parallel private education

(juku).[1] In some countries, experiments with 'vouchers' seem to have brought about the same result. Where supplementary schooling is not possible and differentiation is refused on principle, adaptation to rising social inequalities in educational opportunity occurs both through a decline in the average level of general education and through school failure. An alternative adaptation method is, clearly, to admit that there is a difference in quality between educational establishments and that the diplomas they award do not have the same value. In such cases, educational failure rates are lower, educational provision is highly hetero-geneous and the conditions under which teaching staff operate differ significantly. The advantage of such a system, as noted particularly in the case of Italy, is that it is more flexible and is based on local conditions. The disadvantage is that, despite formal equal recognition of diplomas by the State, everyone knows that they are not comparable and that opportunities differ depending on where one lives.

129. Members of the Study Group take differing views on the importance of the issue of inequalities of educational opportunity and social cohesion, but all agree that:

- it is essential to offer good quality general education to the greatest possible number;

- where conditions permit, the ideal would be for schools to continue to act as a social crucible, i.e. that children from different backgrounds and circumstances have the opportunity to enjoy the same kind of education and to benefit from the same organisational frameworks and programmes of study. The differences between children's back-grounds and circumstances (social or otherwise) demand consider-able organisational and professional effort in order that the principle of equal opportunity is maintained, especially in the pre-school and primary education sectors, where implementation is most important. This demands, in turn, a large increase in the human and financial resources allocated to pre-school and primary education. From this point of view, demographic trends offer a positive opportunity for staff redeployment in favour of those sectors;

---

[1] According to a report from the National Education General Inspectorate, 'Examinations in Europe, the United States and Japan' (Paris, March 1994), in 1992, a good juku cost 300,000 yen per year (approx. ECU 2,160) for 9 hours per week during the evening or weekend. On average, 36% of pupils take part in supplementary education. The distribution by sector is: 8% in kindergarten, 39% in primary, 66% in lower secondary (preparing for selection for upper secondary) and 21% in upper secondary.

- where children do not reach satisfactory levels of achievement, greater flexibility should be considered. One option would be to re-examine the issue of the practice of repeating the year.[1] Another option would be specific forms of setting which use different methods of teaching and learning, but which do not preclude rejoining standard classes and tracks at a later stage. In today's Europe, 'moving up into the next class' year by year in primary schooling is automatic in some countries (Denmark, Ireland, Sweden and the UK). In other Member States, staying another year at the same level is possible for those pupils having difficulties.[2] Furthermore, working methods at school need to be looked at more closely as far as rectifying underachievement is concerned, and more resources must be allocated for children with special needs.

- where these strategies do not work, there must be no hesitation in considering specific systems of special support, but which also enable children to rejoin standard schools and programmes at a later stage;

- in any event, the Study Group considers that, regardless of the means used, the consolidation of democratisation in education rests on a **guarantee to all young Europeans that they will finish compulsory schooling[3] with a foundation of recognised basic knowledge and skills.** The purpose is not to stop the possibility of large numbers of young people from entering post-compulsory education. The purpose is rather to ensure that all adolescents have the resources to face the world around them and to be able subsequently to develop their skills throughout life by different means, including self-teaching. Given current school failure rates, the significant level of absenteeism in certain secondary schools, all the observations made in the next paragraph with regard to vocational training, and the nature of the handicaps facing many young people at the age of 20, it is not a question of a recommended minimum level. On the contrary, the guarantee noted above is an extremely ambitious aim which, if achieved in the coming years, will constitute significant progress towards the democratisation of education.

---

[1] 'Peut-on combattre l'échec scolaire?' by Marcel Crahay, Université de Liège, ed. De Boeck, 1996.

[2] Key Data on Education in the European Union '95, Map D1: progress through primary schooling, academic year 1994/5, annex 9.

[3] The age at which compulsory schooling ends differs between Member States, rising to 18 in some countries; therefore, flexibility is required in the interpretation of this proposal.

**Carte D1. Going up into the next class during Primary Education
Academic year 1994-1995.**

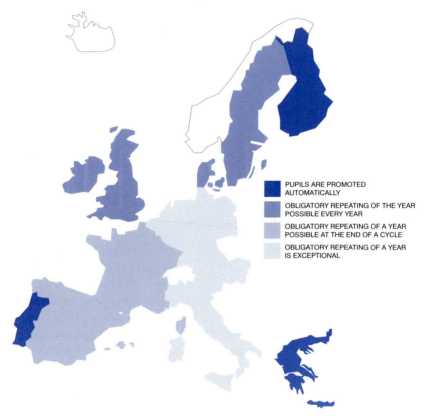

PUPILS ARE PROMOTED
AUTOMATICALLY

OBLIGATORY REPEATING OF THE YEAR
POSSIBLE EVERY YEAR

OBLIGATORY REPEATING OF A YEAR
POSSIBLE AT THE END OF A CYCLE

OBLIGATORY REPEATING OF A YEAR
IS EXCEPTIONAL

*Source:* Key data on education in the European Union, 1995 Edition.

130. The development of vocational training is also a decisive factor in consolidating the democratisation of education. Today, all the Member States have a wide range of training options to meet the requirements both of the labour market and of individuals themselves, and to encourage continuing vocational training. Publicly funded initial vocational training programmes for young people have also undergone significant development, in both school-based systems (France, Sweden and Finland) and in practice-oriented systems (Germany, the Netherlands, Denmark and the UK), which also include 'off-the-job' training in technical colleges or vocational educational establishments. Training provision for adults is very diverse; here the private sector plays a considerable role, and individual initiative, in general, predominates. Local and regional levels still play an important role in this field of vocational training.

The difficulty would seem to lie with the number of training organisations (nearly 60,000 in Europe), which means that there is little transparency in the market. The challenges today are, clearly, to extend a wide palette of training opportunities to all age groups, and to take account of new forms of paid work, particularly part-time work and self-employment. Finally, a major requirement is for training to play more of a proactive than a reactive role (for instance, retraining plans for the unemployed) for the entire workforce. At the moment, forward-looking training that aims to prepare in advance for changes in occupational and task activities is still almost exclusively restricted to management. Nevertheless, in some countries considerable progress has been made: for example, in August 1996 the Swedish government announced that in the next five years, significant efforts will be made to promote adult education.

## Introducing new methods of social integration

131. The Study Group considers that four key questions must be given immediate priority. The way in which we deal with these questions will be decisive for the establishment of a new social integration model. They are: (i) pre-school education; (ii) guidance at the end of compulsory schooling and on entry to university; (iii) specific methods for dealing with the socially excluded and with the prevention of social exclusion; (iv) lifelong learning.

## The vital importance of educating children as early as possible

132. The age at which formal education begins varies between the Member States of the European Union. All are agreed, however, that the early childhood experience has a determining influence on personality development and subsequent social integration. For this reason, pre-school education and 'early start' programmes for young children — with equal consideration given to girls and boys — are increasingly popular. The changing role of the family as a social institution often means that parents (or a parent) are no longer at home full time. Crèches and nursery schools have been increasingly called upon to fill the gap. A number of European countries offer good quality pre-school provision, other countries less so. The relatively well-off can use good quality private nursery education for their children to replace the education and socialisation work that they themselves have not been able to provide. In contrast, poor families and dysfunctional families cannot offer a good early education, which makes social integration more difficult later on. These

101

families either do not have the necessary resources or they do not appreciate the importance of early education. Therefore, no action will be taken unless the community intervenes. In this situation, the gap between children — who (usually) come from the middle or upper classes, who receive family support and follow the standard educational trajectory — and the others quickly becomes significant. In time, it can be assumed that this will lead to school failure and to alienation. In effect, there are numerous studies — in particular, in 1995 the Commission recently published the report *The importance of pre-school education in the European Union: a survey of the question* in its Education Studies, No. 6 — that show the essential question to be one of examining how pre-school education provision can complement and support families in the education of their children.

133. All governments in the European Union must give serious consideration and support to the question of pre-school education. There are great divergencies between countries here: the average period during which a child attends an educational establishment prior to beginning compulsory primary schooling can vary between one year to more than three years. [1]

**Graph C4: Average duration of pre-school education, 1992/93**

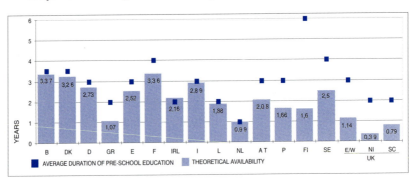

*Source:* see Annex.

**Ireland**: The calculation of the average duration of pre-school attendance includes some 6- and 7-year-olds, of compulsory school age, who are in the 'infant classes'.
**Luxembourg**: Since 1993, the theoretical duration available is three years.
**Netherlands**: The first optional year of the *Basisonderwijs* is considered a pre-school year.

EXPLANATORY NOTE

*The average duration of pre-school education is obtained by adding the rates of pre-school attendance for the various ages. For example, in Belgium, 38% of 2-year-olds + 97.6% of 3-year-olds + 99.2% of 4-year-olds + 97.8 % of 5-year-olds + 4.0% of 6-year-olds giving 336.6, or 3.37 years.*

---

[1] Key Data on Education in the European Union '95, Graph C4: average duration of pre-schooling, academic year 1992/3, annex 10.

Furthermore, carefully designed intervention programmes should be developed to assist parents, particularly where conditions are unfavourable, to encourage good school-family relations. The aim is that these parents gain an awareness of their children's needs, and that they themselves become better educated — and therefore better educators of their children. There is a close link between a poor start and school failure. Early attention to this would be a true investment in the development of human resources, although the return on that investment would be neither immediate nor easy to assess.

134. Extra support outside school hours for pupils in difficulties is one option. This support can be provided by voluntary/community associations or from voluntary educators supported by local authorities and communities. This system has proved very effective in the countries where it has been applied, particularly Denmark. In this case, the community takes over responsibility for certain shortcomings in families. Here, too, some flexibility is required in order to mobilise educational resources in a given area. This flexibility does not generally exist in countries where the doctrine of the 'single school' and of the monopoly of public sector schools predominates. A simple and particularly effective way of preventing the development of such community support systems is to stipulate that all voluntary educators must hold a national diploma for the teaching subject in question. In this instance, the corporate interest clearly obstructs the process of rectifying educational inequality.

## Guidance

135. Guidance is necessary at two key stages: after the end of compulsory schooling, in order to choose between vocational training or further education tracks, and when entering university. All European countries have introduced systems to provide guidance and information on occupations and on how to enter them. In some countries, specialist bodies of counsellors have been established. The members of the Study Group feel that teachers themselves should become more involved in guidance. This presupposes that they receive training in guidance and that they can 'decode' vocational pathways and can identify their vocations. It would also be worthwhile for leading companies in a sector to participate in regular meetings held at schools, so that they can describe developments in the occupations which they have to offer. Finally, effective vocational guidance and

counselling should ensure that girls in particular do not restrict themselves (or are automatically guided towards) typically female-staffed occupations, because, on the whole, these do not offer good career prospects.

136. We must acknowledge that current uncertainties about occupational trends and labour market opportunities are an obstacle to the effectiveness of guidance. It therefore appears essential to follow the recommendations made earlier with regard to highlighting 'generic occupations' and 'occupational profiles', which would, in addition, have the advantage of modifying a certain number of social connotations which disadvantage pupils, notably those in difficulty. After all, even well-informed adults are in no position to tell 16 or 17-year olds which path they should take, given their potential and preferences. Young people today should try to design a personal-professional project, which may change subsequently, but which enables them to see that education and training are long-term investments. This is also a way of developing a sense of individual responsibility in education and training choices, a responsibility which must be exercised throughout one's life. Finally, the main advantage of sustained action in favour of guidance and counselling is to change a number of social connotations which disadvantage pupils, particularly those who are in difficulty. Guidance should give them the ambition to open up horizons which, in certain contexts, would not naturally come to mind.

137. At the end of compulsory schooling, guidance should make it possible to choose a field of study. Where possible, these choices should relate to tracks of equivalent quality and be easily reversible. This presupposes a number of 'bridges' between these tracks and more highly developed equivalent modular systems. Tendencies of corporate protectionism to over-compartmentalise disciplines should be resisted. The same should apply to universities. The choice of a subject in a wider group of disciplines (law in social sciences, for example) should allow for the possibility of changing fields. This is less and less the case. Here, too, the only justification for this compartmentalisation is a form of corporatist protectionism. Both the need to liberate knowledge and the fundamental logic of the development of research argue in favour of increasing the number of bridges and equivalencies. This would allow the development of multiskilling both in the vocational sense and in the sense of key transferable skills at several levels.

# Specific treatment of the socially excluded

138. Europe has experienced difficult adjustments in the last decade. This has resulted in large numbers of people, and particularly young people, who do not have useful qualifications and who are unemployed. They are dependent upon social benefits of various kinds; they may be on training courses and schemes, but with uncertain future prospects. These people, who have considerable difficulties, generally live in the disadvantaged areas of our large cities. Local authorities, central governments and voluntary or community associations have made considerable efforts to alleviate the situation. The Study Group considers that the young unqualified, [1] whose family and social backgrounds and circumstances are least likely to offer opportunities for their future, are the most urgent problem to be addressed. Rising criminality and drug abuse are direct consequences of this situation.

139. If we do not give immediate and specific priority to these young people, in the long term we will consolidate the idea that our societies accept an irreducible hard-core of people in this situation. This will clearly be a step backwards in social terms, which will ultimately call into question the construction of Europe itself. It should also be borne in mind that important as education and training initiatives are in seeking to resolve problems of social exclusion, such measures on their own will not be sufficient. Intersectoral interventions should be envisaged whereby educational initiatives are supplemented by co-operative action in such areas as housing, health, social welfare, employment and justice.

140. In its White Paper *Teaching and learning*, the Commission proposed experimental projects to develop a 'second chance through school' with the aim of adopting them on a general scale. Above all, these projects should show that, with sufficient resources, suitable teaching and learning methods and the mobilisation of all private and public operators in a major conurbation, it is possible to put these young people back on the path towards integration, or even success. This venture cannot be allowed to fail, because many think that this population group is beyond help and that all that society can do in future is support them by means of benefits and control their excesses through police action. Everything indicates that this is not true, even for those who have used economically illegal means to survive.

---

[1] Key Data on Education in the European Union '95, Graph A8: unemployment and educational level, unemployment rate for 25 to 35 year olds by educational level, 1993, annex 11.

## Graph A8: Unemployment and level of education Unemployment rates (%) for people aged 25 to 35 by level of education, 1993

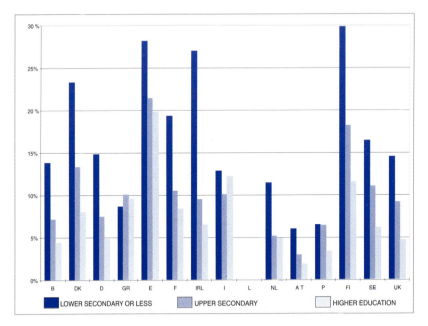

Source: Eurostat, Labour force survey.

**Luxembourg**: Data not available.
**Sweden**: Data provided by the national statistical office.

---

EXPLANATORY NOTE

*The Eurostat labour force survey provides statistical information with regard to employment and unemployment in the European Union. The data are obtained from large scale sample surveys, which are carried out annually by the statistical offices of the Member States. The methods of data collection are devised to obtain statistical information which is optimally comparable both between countries and across years.*

*Lower secondary education corresponds to ISCED 2 under the Unesco International Standard Classification for Education, upper secondary education to ISCED 3 and higher education to ISCED 5 (higher non-university education), 6 (first university degree or equivalent) and 7 (second-stage — post-graduate — university degree or equivalent).*

---

141. With the needs of these kinds of people in mind, the activities and experiments of the kind referred to immediately above have now become a priority. The principles that guide these actions should be as follows: (i) these people must be integrated into ambitious programmes that aim for excellence and do not simply provide supportive or compensatory social measures; (ii) teaching and learning methods must be completely transformed, or turned upside down;[1] these methods must begin from

---

[1] St. Ignatius Loyola, speaking of education, said that 'similar illnesses do not always have to be treated in a similar way; but depending on the kind of illness, we may have to use different remedies and even entirely opposite ones'.

the behavioural skills that such young people already possess. Having identified those skills, the aim is to develop them further, but with the ultimate purpose of offering a specific perspective for the learners' future. Methods of teaching and learning must also consolidate the foundation of essential basic knowledge; and finally, they must accredit competencies, and not always necessarily with 'pieces of paper'; (iii) action must be taken on a continuous basis and begin very early indeed in order to prevent school failure; (iv) support from the business sector must be secured from the outset; (v) support from local organisations, in particular from universities, must be secured; (vi) this support would mean that, if possible, young highly disadvantaged people have university students as mentors (through European Voluntary Service); and that new kinds of higher education courses are developed for this new potential clientele, just as the vocational training system and voluntary/community associations cater to their needs today.

142. The experimental projects referred to earlier are necessarily limited in scope. But they can 'fertilise' other support programmes for such young people. These projects can give young people new educational horizons, erasing the effects of their experiences with traditional or standard teaching and learning methods and courses. Above all, these projects can explicitly prove that those young people who come from different cultural backgrounds and who have not succeeded in gaining a formal qualification by the age of 20 are not incapable of playing a positive role in the development of our society. Implementing special measures of this kind may be criticised because they are not immediately available to all highly disadvantaged young people and because they might become 'ghettos' before they can achieve a reputation for excellence. In response to the first criticism, the answer lies in the level of resources made available. More resources would enable more such projects. In response to the second criticism, it can be said that these young people are already in ghettos — but in ghettos with no exits.

## Lifelong learning

143. If lifelong learning becomes an aim fully adopted by governments and takes on tangible form, the coming years will become a benchmark in the history of education. Lifelong learning (LLL) holds the potential to change the public's entire understanding of education. It will provide

an awareness that education and training are continuing processes, without, however, being diverted from the need to make special efforts for younger people. Many analyses of contemporary and future social and cultural models underline the need for this wide, all-encompassing view of education as a developing, lifelong process. Modern society will be a learning society, and Europe will have a dominant place in that society if this educational concept is fully developed. Lifelong learning can bring together all aspects of educational thinking and policy-making; early childhood education, 'second chance' education, adult education, community education and traditional education itself.

144. The question of how to implement LLL remains. There are a number of possibilities. The first is that employers and/or governments enable people to take paid 'education leave'. The second places more trust in individual responsibility by offering easily accessible databases for different types of knowledge and accreditation, particularly on the basis of distance university learning. This direction, which provides more room for individual responsibility, requires the development of a universally accessible 'supermarket' of educational products (courses and accreditation). The third possibility is to insist on codified rights to continuing education, either at national or industry level, with the necessary budgetary resources. Whatever the solution or combination of solutions chosen, it should be pointed out that the information technologies which are bringing about far-reaching changes in our societies simultaneously provide the means to achieve LLL. The general development of information technologies and new media offers an unprecedented opportunity to implement it: **henceforth, education and training could be possible for the entire population, anywhere and at any time when this is technically possible.**

## Guidelines for action in Europe

145. Europe's future prospects could lead to three main areas for European-level action: (i) help provide guarantees to all young Europeans that they will learn and acquire a foundation of essential basic skills; (ii) help to facilitate guidance and counselling at critical·moments of transition; (iii) develop experiments that aim to support, popularise and disseminate pre-school education and the struggle against social exclusion.

# A foundation of essential basic knowledge at the end of compulsory education for all young Europeans

146. It is now of decisive importance to meet this aim, because failure at school is the cause of all future ills. The method chosen by each educational system in order to achieve it is of little importance; it is the outcome that is important.[1] The Study Group considers this to be the most important recommendation for maintaining social cohesion in Europe. It might be considered a *priori* that this foundation should include: the maths and science level necessary at this age; the ability to

**Graph E1: Ages at which compulsory full-time education and the first cycle of secondary education are completed, 1994/95**

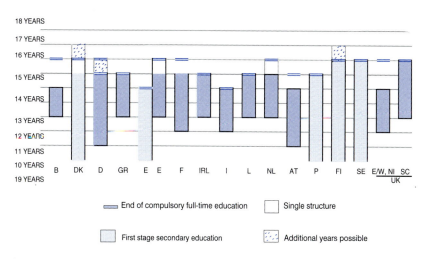

*Source:* Key data on education in the European Union, 1995 Edition.

**Germany**: The duration of full-time compulsory education is nine years in 12 *Länder* and 10 years in four. It therefore ends at age 15 or age 16.

---

### EXPLANATORY NOTE

*The International Standard Classification for Education (ISCED), developed by Unesco, is used by countries and international agencies as a means of compiling internationally comparable statistics on education.*

*In accordance with this classification, the last three years of 'basic education' in Spain (pre-reform) and the Folkeskole (Denmark), of the Ensino básico in Portugal, of the Peruskoulu/Grundskola (Finland), and of the Grundskola (Sweden) are considered to be of the same level as the first stage of secondary education (ISCED 2).*

---

[1] Key Data on Education in the European Union '95, Graph E1: age at the end of full-time compulsory education and at the end of the first cycle of secondary education, academic year 1994/5, annex 12 (the end of the first cycle secondary education or of basic comprehensive education often corresponds to the age at which compulsory full-time education ends.

work on a computer screen; reading; writing; history and civics; and a basic knowledge of a foreign language. The question of content, however, is open and should be the subject of joint discussion by the different Member States. While it might be possible to establish European-wide standards, European-wide examinations are clearly not the way to validate young people's achievement levels. Instead, tests could be offered to all European educational institutions — or to each individual — who would be free to make use of them or not.

147. Achieving this would involve:

- European-level meetings between national programme committees to define the content and nature of this foundation;

- wide availability of systems for the accreditation of skills in order to make it possible, **where necessary**, to verify acquisition of this foundation;

- indexing and dissemination of the best educational practices available among the Member States for acquiring this foundation;

- publication of manuals and multimedia tools devoted to the attainment of this objective. A degree of caution is required here, because this foundation should not become the standard expectation for achievement after the age of 16. Many children should go beyond this. Preference should be given to the use of informal types of assessment, which do not affect opportunities to pursue further education or particular subjects and tracks. These assessments can be conducted by educational establishments or by pupils themselves. The system of accreditation of skills proposed in the White Paper action guidelines could in time provide, along with other systems, validation possibilities.

## Facilitating guidance

148. Europe is an appropriate level from which to assist with guidance measures carried out in the Member States. This presupposes that:

- work carried out to identify generic skills and new occupational profiles is transferred to schools and to those responsible for giving guidance and counselling to pupils;

- a permanent information system covering fields of education, universities and areas of training is introduced at European level;

- teaching staff find it easier to move into the world of business;

- more use is made of the major media (particularly television);

- events such as European job and skills fairs are organised, and that efforts are made to facilitate the communication of and access to available data on employment and occupations, and on the skills required.

## Developing targeted support experiments

149. Europe should be able to use its major programmes, particularly Leonardo and Socrates, to carry out specific experimental projects. Member States have the choice to implement such experiments on a wider basis, if they wish to do so. These projects could be aimed at disseminating good practice, particularly in pre-school and primary education and for combatting social exclusion. Community education and training action programmes present a privileged means for doing so. It would be necessary to achieve a balance in the allocation of available funding, thus reserving a given proportion for highly innovative projects (for example, between one-quarter and one-fifth of the total sum available) and the remainder for projects which aim to disseminate results and to transfer good practice. The effectiveness and the impact of Community-level action could thus be improved and rendered more pertinent in that it addresses the problems posed by the construction of the learning society. Projects can concentrate on a number of interlinked problems at the same time. With this in mind, experiments should be attempted, or extended, to cover:

- forms of pre-school and primary support outside school hours which involve local authorities and associations, particularly by trying to transfer the best practices into other contexts;

- support for informal education systems that enable the development of lifelong learning (particularly knowledge exchange networks and adult/community education services);

- second-chance measures, diversified in national and local contexts, directed to formally unqualified and socially excluded young people to return to learning processes which the learning society makes necessary.

# V. Education and training in the information society

150. The new information technologies are a source of both concern and fascination. After the informatics revolution, they open up new, apparently unlimited possibilities for human communication. The integration between different communication media will probably change our environment to an even more significant extent. Education and training cannot stay on the sidelines. They will have to redefine their role and become a decisive element in optimising the use of these technologies.

## Towards a new approach to education and training

151. Undoubtedly, the exponential development of new information technologies (IT) will lead to profound transformations in education and training. Some even talk of a new paradigm which will overturn educational process and methods, educational actors' roles and positions, and even the concept of education itself[1]. At the moment, no-one can predict the direction these changes will take, and how they will affect education and training. In the first place, in opening up all sorts of possibilities, IT represents major industrial and cultural challenges. This prompts struggles for power, which have yet to be played out. In the second place, all ultimately depends on the way in which users approach IT and the opportunities they are offered to appropriate the potential of IT. In the third place, the response of educational systems to IT remains uncertain.

152. Major educational philosophers consider that any process of acquiring and constructing knowledge, or even knowledge itself,[2] is dependent on the historical, social and cultural context in which people produce it. If this is so, then it appears that considerable changes are about to take place.

---

[1] Cf. 'The educational paradigm shift', report of the Task Force of the International Council on Distance Education, Standing Committee of Presidents, June 1996.

[2] Cf. Emmanuel Kant 'The critique of pure reason'.

The main change will arise from the fact that learners will continuously choose and modify their own educational process. Learners will enter into a dialogue with a succession of speakers or voices, where the 'formal' voice (school, university, etc.) will be only one among many. At random, learners will access a multitude of sources and encounter a mass of available information, which together comprise representations of scientific, human or social reality. In addition, this information will come from a range of cultural and national sources. To interpret this information, learners will require an understanding of its originating cultures. Finally, the use of time and space will no longer be the same. This educational process will take place outside a classroom, at times other than during the academic year or term, and certainly throughout one's life.

153. Among the potential changes identified,[1] the following should be noted:

- the transition from objective to constructed knowledge;

- the transition from an industrial to a learning society;

- the change in educational mission from instruction to the provision of methods for personal learning;

- the increasing (and perhaps, in the future, dominant) role of technology in the communication process and in knowledge acquisition;

- the shift away from formal educational institutions such as schools and universities towards organisational structures for learning which have yet to be determined.

154. The Study Group considers that these developments will take place more slowly than certain current hypotheses would suppose. Technological innovations become social innovations necessarily as slowly as the capacities of organisations and individuals are able to assimilate them. There will probably be a relatively long interim period before IT is widely introduced into schools and begins to play a major part in household consumer budgets, as is the case with personal computers and the use of information networks and electronic communication (only 5% of European schools are connected to Internet, and teleworking currently concerns only 1% of employees). In addition, despite a clear decline in the cost of IT apparatus, their speed of development means that they rapidly become obsolescent and depreciate. This already dissuades

---

[1] In particular by the International Council on Distance Education.

purchase by private households, as with the personal computer. It is very likely, therefore, that businesses and the vocational training sector will be involved initially. The main danger which the Study Group wishes to emphasise is the risk of unequal access to these new media, reserving them for the employed and more affluent social milieux. Allowances should be made immediately for this risk, so that collective access channels can be introduced as quickly as possible, for example, resource centres, equipment in public libraries.

155. Nevertheless, IT presents a considerable challenge for education and training systems. Today, many take the view that the era of school-based education is coming to a close. This will liberate educational process and will place more control in the hands of those providers that are more innovative than traditional educational structures. The Study Group's view is a more positive one. There will be no substitute for school, nor for the human relationship established between pupil and teacher. No form of virtual technology, and no automatic system, will ever attain the richness and intelligence of direct human communication. It may even be that human communication will take on an added value once the limitations of the communications by technology are realised.

Certain experiences, in particular those developed at local level, tend to show that schools and teachers could play a pivotal role in integrating their environment and their locality into Information Society networks. As communication and knowledge access specialists, teachers themselves are in a position not only to furnish their environment with the keys of access to networks and the intellectual means to make good use of the available information, but also to participate more intensively in including locally organised community networks into wider and more generalised networks. It would be interesting to discover whether such activities on the part of teachers will take place within institutional school frameworks or rather on the margins or alongside these.

156. The worlds of education and training must, however, take advantage of the considerable opportunity offered by these new information technologies; not only by using them, but by taking part in their development. The Study Group considers that IT provides a means to improve education: (i) by freeing teachers from numerous less central tasks, IT helps to make space for the development of more important and challenging elements of teaching practice, especially pedagogy; (ii) by improving teaching and learning methods, for example, in expanding access to data and multimedia simulations and in introducing objective assessments that are immediately accessible to the learner; (iii) by encouraging individual and

small group work; (iv) by encouraging the world of education to open itself up to the community, to review its relationship with pupils and to participate in lifelong learning. Finally, what is at stake is also important for Europe. It is doubtful whether our continent will take its rightful place in this new market if our education and training systems do not rapidly respond to the challenge. The development of these technologies, in the context of strong international competition, requires that the effects of scale play their full part. If the world of education and training does not use IT, Europe will become a mass market too late. The transformation of education and training as described earlier will then be shaped by other players.

## Favouring a pro-active education and training approach to new information technologies

157. Differences between ways of learning have been summarised in the epithet that 'We take in 20% of what we see, 40% of what we see and hear, and 70% of what we see, hear and do ourselves'. If this is true, a combination of computers, networking arrangements, and multimedia technology is clearly a formidable educational tool.

158. As a 'teacher', the computer is accurate, expert, instant in response, available, and objective and unbiased as regards gender, race, religion, appearance, health, sexual orientation, learning level or learning pace. As a 'library', computerised information networks already provide *practicably* instant world-wide access to almost unimaginable depth of information. As a *virtual learning* 'club', computerised networks offer the potential of world-wide networking with individuals with similar specialised interest, for example community groups; remote access to tutors *and* other students in what would be a virtual community of learners; or perhaps of more interest in a European education context, allow in-depth instant interaction between schools and colleges in different Member States.

159. Modern information technology is pervasive in everyday life at work, even if there remains important progress to be made in order to involve all educational institutions in this process. Once at work students will be expected to be able to learn through their own efforts, through hands-on experimentation through their computer, and relatively little through formal tuition in a group context. The world of State education needs to keep pace both with the world of work and with the competitive private sector market in IT-based learning packages. This is especially true if State education is to appeal to young people through being modern and

relevant to their present and future existence. This does not mean training young people how to use the computer or access the networks, important though these are, but the much more radical step of delivering all or most of the curriculum through this mode in a fully integrated way.

160. The education process also needs to engender in individuals a capacity to manage their own learning process and an eagerness to continue with lifelong learning if Europe is to achieve the skill levels and rates of adaptation required to become competitive. This requires flexible learning methods (not necessarily computer-based), to allow the individual to control the time and pace of their learning. This applies for people of all ages, but particularly in schools it is necessary to encourage pupils to access work stations outside of normal lesson hours, and without supervision. Use of IT is appropriate to the extent that it is cost-effective, and this needs to be reviewed regularly because the power of IT is growing exponentially while the real cost of IT systems is falling gradually. IT is therefore likely to have a vital role in achieving step increases in participation in post compulsory education in a cost-effective way, as well as in increasing the effectiveness and depth of compulsory education itself. Studies in Member States and in the US confirm both effectiveness and productivity of teaching can be improved, especially in mathematics.

161. Providing individual learning modes is important for lifelong learning and is especially important as a tool with which to overcome exclusion of various sorts (e.g. rural dispersion, people with disabilities, people at home caring for children or elderly relatives, people lacking the confidence to learn in a group or to travel to group education). Individual lifelong learning opportunities are also especially important for women, who are still much more likely to have childcare and eldercare responsibilities which often make it difficult for them to participate in education and training courses offered in the traditional manner. It is also important for the increasing group of part-time and casual/fixed contract employees together with those on self-employed or subsidiary contracts, since here, employers have less incentive to invest in skills and development. The empowerment of the individual and the opening and widening of access to learning are therefore critical aspects of potential of IT from the point of view of European policy and strategy.

162. Given these needs for relevant modern flexible access to individually tailored learning, what can IT offer? What are the advantages? What are the drawbacks?

163. The advantages of IT media are the fact that they are good fun, easy to use and can be put to continuous and repetitive use. They can be used anywhere at any time and allow the learner to establish the pace, accelerating through or skipping the known or familiar and focusing, pausing, repeating the new or the difficult. They allow networking with remote fellow students and mentoring from remote tutors. All these features mean, in addition, that IT is often highly empowering for the physically handicapped and for those with learning difficulties. IT media bring world databases to the learner's elbow. What is more, this is a dynamic and growing sector both from the point of view of products and of cost, being dominated by private providers.

164. IT can encourage choice by opening up an alternative learning route (e.g. to study to baccalaureate level at home via guided independent study) or by remote accessing of experts in specialist subjects which the average school/college cannot afford. IT can be used to simulate real-life situations, something which greatly facilitates training. One can simulate, for example, in physics and chemistry. This goes much further than the well known and very costly use in simulating catastrophic crises (e.g. avoiding aeroplane accidents). In particular, simulation with multimedia and virtual reality enables the world to be brought into the classroom or the living-room at home. This enables a living culture to be brought to the individual, e.g. to explore great buildings in virtual reality or to create orchestral music on one's own. Although IT is no panacea, effectiveness in an educational environment is undisputed.

165. On the downside, IT may give rise to misuse. The protection of minors must be assured with respect to electronic information networks just as for all other media, whilst preserving individual freedom of expression. It is imperative to adopt a code of good practice at international level which covers the use of global information networks if IT media are to be educationally employed. Furthermore, teaching staff must be properly briefed on the all-round benefits the wide-spread use of IT can bring as part of a redesigned pedagogical approach. It may create divisions and a kind of underclass of those who have no access. In addition, the most vulnerable people may be led to turn in on themselves if the technologies are incorrectly perceived to exclude such factors as friendship, leadership, team working or to be incompatible with physical activities such as sport. Finally the flavour of most software does not reflect European taste or culture; it is important that as IT quickly becomes the world-wide channel for communication that European influences as well as American values and approaches are reflected.

118

The Study Group has addressed — without being able to go into real depth — the question of the content of educational multimedia tools and the necessity of defining the modes of market regulation, with respect to the protection of the consumer and the individual. However, the Group underlines the fact that these regulations cannot take the form of control and censorship 'before the event', but are better founded in rules of etiquette and behaviour. The Group considers that this theme deserves immediate closer attention and that the Union could take initiatives in this domain.

166. Nonetheless, the benefits greatly outweigh the disadvantages, provided IT is properly utilised and supported. Within compulsory education it should probably be seen as complementary to traditional teaching, and in post-compulsory rarely would be completely adequate alone. The policy should be to help young people to make proper use of the available technologies. The resistance to their use in public education systems probably stems from social factors and capital budget constraints. The natural resistance of the traditional public system will need to be overcome by a combination of encouragement, goals, resources, consumer orientation and competition from the private sector. **It might also be necessary to create, at European or national levels, a public sector virtual competitor to complement other public provision, i.e. a virtual school, college or university, at least in subjects or at levels where private sector competition is either inadequate or only available to the better-off.**

The relative failure of some attempts to equip schools massively with informatics equally shows that such efforts must be accompanied by training policies for teachers and trainers, a matter which is often neglected. From this point of view, the next stage of equipping schools with information transfer networks points to giving a much more significant role to teacher training.

Henceforth, state, regional or local education authorities should:

(i) achieve the cost-effective optimal use of multimedia and traditional learning approaches;

(ii) ensure that all teachers and students have appropriate skills to assess the utility of and operate IT-assisted approaches;

(iii) make available to all pupils and students, including adults, learning opportunities which make optimal use of all learning methodologies.

# Implementation policy

167. Policy implementation must therefore focus on the following points:

- facilitating access from public libraries and resource centres, and providing systematic facilities in public educational establishments, to ensure that use is not restricted to the employed and the well-off. The generalised use of the requisite equipment will make it possible for people to have access to network arrangements, to learn, to access information, to assess their own progress, to gain accreditation for their achievements, to educate themselves and simply to know;

- demystifying the practical use of IT for teachers and adults, in particular mobilising and reforming initial teacher training and continuing professional development;

- appropriately equipping all educational establishments with modern hardware and permit their access to information networks;

- introducing more learner-centred approaches;

- accrediting informally acquired knowledge;

- applying IT to all stages of the traditional learning process, e.g. initial deliveries, revision, supervision, relieving the teacher of purely mechanical chores, helping in the assessment process, and even funding IT implementation through productivity gains achieved at all stages of the learning process;

- giving consideration to the development of educational software rooted in European culture to be available as a public good in state education systems, perhaps initially in key subjects such as mathematics, science, information technology itself and languages;

- make greater use of IT in the training of adults whether employed or unemployed;

- bringing specific provision to girls and women, in order to equalise their IT access and skills;

- defining quality standards in order that IT may be used constructively and giving teachers the necessary education and training for debating and mastering ethical and moral problems concerning the use of IT;

- making use of R&D experience with respect to IT in education and training;

- helping teachers to devote more time to the methodological aspects and less to the technical aspects;

- encouraging software that develops creativity and problem-solving, allowing the learner to be the content-provider and not simply conveying information and techniques;

- experimenting on a trial basis with the use of IT to bring together resourcing of learning opportunities with their delivery and with their assessment and recording their outcome, e.g., personal records of achievement.

168. As IT — understood as tools and methods and not as a 'subject' in itself — comes into more general use in mainstream education, there is a need to bring about changes in attitudes and to acquire the necessary equipment for schools and universities. We shall also have to promote the technologies among families and with parents and young people, some of whom may find learning with less human teacher contact disconcerting. At the same time we must be vigilant as to product quality and the results obtained. Looked at from this angle, the creation at European level of a skills accreditation system will be an important means of keeping a check on the skills really being acquired via IT. Whether there is a need or 'space' for a European-wide development of educational software for 3-21 but available to all ages, is an issue that deserves further urgent examination.

169. Finally, many of these ideas about the potential of IT in education and training are not new.[1] What is needed is concerted action by the Commission and by Member States on the key priorities.

---

[1] See: Bangemann report on the Information Society; Task Force Educational Software and Multimedia report, European Commission (DG XIII and DG XXII), July 1996; the first annual report of the Information Society Forum, June 1996; and the European Commission action plan Learning in the Information Society, September 1996.

# VI. Making education and training systems more dynamic and giving support to the players

## A complex problem

170. The preceding chapters have described the challenges facing our education and training systems. They also make it clear that responding to such challenges is crucial for society itself. Is it fair to accuse education and training systems of failing to resolve those very questions that our societies themselves find most difficult to address? Here are just some of those difficult questions:

- What balance have we found between the demand for economic and technological competitiveness and the need for social cohesion? At the moment the answer is far from clear-cut. Would it be better to focus our efforts on promoting the most dynamic human resource elements in order to win the global competition, and then to compensate the losers as far as our budgets allow? Or should we plan to 'repair' initial inequalities of background and circumstance, to reject the notion of an irreducible core of social exclusion and to seek to arrange social conditions in more open — and possibly less competitive — ways? It is obvious that we need more and better quality — but quality for what? Quality that enables selection of the ever-smaller numbers of pupils required by the labour market? Or quality for all, but which does not guarantee a job? The various education systems within Europe have clearly made their choice. The first option — promoting winners and compensating losers — means the encouragement both of the schools and universities that perform best and of those education and training tracks that correspond most closely to labour market demand. It implies concentrating the development of quality and innovation within those education and training establishments, and turning the rest into 'parking lots' of varying organisational efficiency. In this case, everyone will know that paper qualifications are not of comparable quality; nationally or officially recognised qualifications will then lose their equality of status and value, even if one maintains their apparently equal value at national level. Taking up this first option, however, implies that the mechanisms used to encourage individual selectivity and institutional differentiation will be both subtle and implicit, because no public powers could openly advocate such policies. The alternative option — quality for all — demands full mobilisation of all resources: more funding, reallocation of funds, positive discrimination measures to rectify negative discrimination against particular age groups and those in the most difficult circumstances.

- Can we really be confident that we are sufficiently in control of technological progress? Are we capable of assimilating that progress into our culture as quickly as needed? Of course, we fully appreciate the demands made on us by the process of globalisation and technological development: occupational, cultural and geographical mobility; the ability to communicate; to review constantly our position; to update our knowledge continuously; to resolve problems, starting with our own. But, apart from a privileged few, how many Europeans are nowadays still locked into their local milieu, their occupation, their status, their employing organisation? The example of the emerging Asian countries and Japan shows that a strong culture and spirit of competition anchored on a cultural bedrock (albeit tempered with unbridled competition between children in general education) constitute an incontestable element of competitiveness. How many prefer the subjectivity of interpersonal relations to the objectivity of business relations and the soulless nature of cyberspace? How can we make it clear to such individuals that personal development, which is at the very heart of the educational mission, means questioning most of our initial assumptions, the very foundation that gives many people their feeling of belonging to society?

- And to go where? Do we currently have a clear idea of the democratic frame of reference which will prevail over the next 20 years? What role will the nation-states, our regions, and Europe itself play in a world that turns ever faster? At which of the above levels should the school slot in — more at national level, for example, or should schooling be more neutral and respect the Community's different ways of life?

171. All these questions cut right across our education systems. Their complexity and the impossibility of giving answers or providing clear guidelines have caused the systems concerned to organise themselves in a manner ensuring a certain amount of durability. The education and

training systems have learned to absorb new ideas from outside and even to change their shape, without fundamentally breaking with their original form even if important changes have appeared. Despite notable changes, the plurality, confusion and often contradictory nature of the messages they receive (as the prevailing political winds change) have sometimes brought education and training systems, perilously close to being completely out of step with societal requirements.

172. If educational systems have become conservative, their players — primarily teachers — are less so, especially in the sense of the development of the profession (but much less so in the sense of changing the system itself). It is teachers who have largely borne the load of mass educational expansion; it is teachers who have supported social relations in the most disadvantaged localities; it is teachers who have, on the whole, maintained quality of learning. Our societies, however, have given little recompense in return. Educational expansion over the past thirty years has led to rising staff numbers: today, the Community has over four million teachers — some 3% of the Union's active population. More flexible staff recruitment procedures have accompanied this expansion, which has, at times, had a negative effect on teacher quality and thus, in certain cases, their social standing — despite the fact that in the shift towards a learning society, the teaching function is a decisive one. At the same time, however, some teachers — university teachers in particular — are increasingly approached by local authorities wishing to draw on their expertise in the social sphere.

173. As far as salaries are concerned — and this is a topic on which more data is needed — three factors account for the changes that have taken place: (i) teachers' salaries have responded negatively to the fall in the relative gap between their formal qualification levels in relation to that of the population average; (ii) teaching overall has been subject to negative status effects of the generalised flattening of salary differentials; (iii) and, as a hypothesis only at this stage, the declining financial rewards of teaching reflect a general fall the productivity levels of educational systems.

174. With some exceptions, internal salary hierarchies in the teaching profession correspond to the level at which teachers are deployed. This means — with the exception of Finland, Italy and Sweden — that primary schoolteachers earn less than secondary schoolteachers. Nevertheless, there are universal trends towards convergence for this indicator, leading to greater similarity of treatment across levels. Whilst in 1965 one could observe almost everywhere a significant difference between primary and

secondary teachers' salaries, by 1993 this pattern had weakened (in Belgium, Spain and Austria) or was at the point of disappearing (in Greece, France, Italy, Finland, Sweden, Ireland and Scotland). Vocational training systems, both as organisations and in terms of staffing, are so diverse that little information is available about trainers' salaries and conditions, so that it is currently impossible to draw a global picture of the situation.

## How can the operation of education and training systems be improved?

175. The Study Group considers that if our education and training systems are to implement the suggestions made in the preceding chapters, there are five things we need to do: (i) make the education and training systems more user-oriented; (ii) increase productivity and effectiveness; (iii) upgrade the jobs of teacher and heads; (iv) introduce evaluation procedures both to encourage reorganisation (the 'mirror effect') and to enable users to make informed choices; (v) be more open to all forms of co-operation

To respond to these briefly sketched imperatives, it would be desirable to draw on the abundant and valuable research conducted in recent decades on school effectiveness, school development, teaching and training methods, educational action on behalf of the disadvantaged, etc., and inform policymakers of their findings. The dissemination of research knowledge combined with practitioner experience will permit the identification and choice of the best implementation strategies for the necessary changes.

## Making education and training systems more user-oriented

176. The education and training systems must be organised better to satisfy the needs of pupils and learners. The education system should be the prime target here. Vocational training systems are already more flexible, less institutionalised, exposed to more competition among themselves and, consequently, more naturally inclined to adapt to their customers.

177. The Study Group considers that transmitting a vision for education is more important than the general formal framework of the system itself, but it is also important to establish a fairly flexible organisation to make the

vision a reality. The vision and the aim is that education should **make it possible to give everyone the opportunity for personal development and for achievement at the high levels required by the new competitive economic context, and also to acquire the personal resources needed for social integration.** [1] Modern trends indicate the need to pay more attention to the top and bottom rungs of the achievement ladder, which are both most directly affected by contemporary developments. This means we need to focus on (i) people with specialist qualifications (of whatever level) who will find themselves competing internationally with their counterparts from other regions of the world, and (ii) those who will be excluded from the learning society because they lack the resources for economic and social integration. This does not imply that those in between do not merit our attention, just that a special effort is needed on the two extremes.

Flexible school organisation implies the abandonment of two presuppositions underlying the majority of educational systems: the social legitimacy of dispensing equal treatment to all learners and the appropriateness of organising learning in homogeneous age-groups. The first idea — that education can only be equitable if it is everywhere identical — is in the process of being demolished in numerous countries; on the other hand, the principle of age — homogenous learning groups — remains common enough. In those educational systems where moving up a class each year is not automatic, a sizeable minority of pupils finds itself, from the lower secondary years onwards, outside the norm because they are not the same age as their classmates. The age criterion was intended to be a rational organisational principle, guaranteeing optimal teaching and learning conditions, but in practice it can become at times a criterion of relegation and exclusion — including self-exclusion — for young people. To move from the logic of the age-group that is thought to be homogenous to the logic of the individual who can follow a partly individualised learning pathway (one which is, above all, differentiated in terms of methods) implies profound internal reform of the existing relations between pupils and the institution and between pupils and teachers.

178. This will require consistent financial inputs from Member States if they wish to attain the above aim via 'the common school', i.e. by offering everyone the same formal framework for achieving it. This appears to

---

[1] This conforms well to the aim held since the Enlightenment: that all children, regardless of their inherent abilities or of family and social circumstance, have the right to access universal knowledge through education.

be feasible at pre-school and primary level, which — as we have already said — is the most crucial stage. If it is not feasible for other stages, or if it is altogether too expensive, then the education system needs to be 'liberated'. Here, too, the formal framework is relatively unimportant. Those countries which have very centralised and state-run systems must provide more opportunities for school-level and teacher-led initiatives, if the nature of the system itself is retained. In Member States whose systems are more decentralised or allow more competition among educational establishments or where private sector education is more developed, it is already more natural to respond to users' needs. The clear danger is that this will encourage an educational elitism which benefits those able to pay; children with special needs end up in state-run schools of inferior quality. In such cases this is where efforts must be focused. Finally, education systems that are decentralised at regional or local level permit optimum adaptation to local conditions and give decision-makers first-hand experience of the social difficulties that young people encounter. This usually means that better account is taken of users' needs. The obvious difficulty here lies in the establishment of co-ordination mechanisms which prevent the emergence of marked regional disparity, and which maintain overall quality. The broader the regions' own powers, the easier this will be, because the regional authorities will necessarily have a more global view.

179. These three forms of organisation already exist in Europe. The Study Group sees no reason to prefer any particular form. In the first place, they are each the fruit of a protracted political and social history. The forms taken by national education systems are therefore very deeply rooted and Member States are quite properly very attached to them. In the second place, each organisational has its good and bad points. Nevertheless, regardless of the organisational form and the kind of decision-making processes adopted in the different educational systems of the European Union, the objectives need to be clearly shared at European level, so that our young people know what we are trying to achieve for them. The past twenty years have seen a notable conver-gence of production costs, relative product prices, currencies and incomes. Yet age-specific educational targets, the teaching and learning methods, curricula and assessment methods have hardly converged at all. This makes no sense. Broad-scale European initiatives are necessary here if we wish to breathe life into the European vision. It is particularly important that at the critical ages (end of compulsory schooling/upper secondary/each university cycle) Europe specifies its aims unambigu-ously and informs all young Europeans where they stand personally, as

well as how their school or college is performing with respect to those aims. This will ensure that our educational establishments pay greater attention to users and to their education as European citizens.

## Increasing productivity and effectiveness

180.  It is not easy to grasp the meaning of productivity and effectiveness in the case of education and training establishments. Any system of measurement is by definition imperfect when applied to establishments themselves. Should one take failure rates as a guideline for funding allocations? Teachers could tend to be less rigorous and pass rates rise considerably. This prompts the media to ask whether paper qualifications obtained have been devalued — some European countries have witnessed this in the past few years. Do we wish to retain quality as a major criterion? Teachers will then seek posts in selective entry schools. This then leads to an explicit hierarchy via salary levels or implicit hierarchy between teachers in selective and non-selective schools. Establishments themselves have always tried to give themselves a special profile by establishing or joining networks that are seen to be prestigious, and which are often non-European (cf developments in connection with business schools at the time of writing this report). A similar situation can be found in continuing training: forward-looking centres (generally focusing on training middle management/executives for major companies) are differentiated from those that respond to public calls to tender for providing training courses that cover population groups in difficulty. Middle management trainers will rarely take a job educating such population groups, because salaries are usually a fifth or a sixth of what they normally earn. Should current pupil-teacher ratios be maintained? This issue invariably leads to a clash between parents and public authorities. Parents always want classes with fewer pupils, because they see this as a sign of good quality (or 'high productivity') teaching and learning. Public authorities use the opposite criterion: they try to close down classes on the grounds that a teacher productivity rises with the number of pupils in the classroom. In addition, discipline-based criteria have led, notably in universities, to never-ending debates between the medical disciplines and 'hard' sciences on the one hand and the social sciences on the other.

181.  Despite all these difficulties, the Study Group considers that the efforts made in the past few years to establish productivity criteria must be continued. This trend implies support for European research on evaluation procedures and the definition of performance criteria. Europe must

contribute to the implementation of these criteria by (i) relating them to clearly defined priorities based on the principles outlined with respect to the search for quality, and (ii) concentrating on the sole incontestable measure of performance, i.e. what pupils or trainees have really learned and how this impacts on their social and working life. Education and training systems will thus be more orientated towards users. In this connection, it is vital that at the critical thresholds, establishments follow up what their pupils go on to do (this practice is still very rare in Europe, universities included).

182. Once these criteria have been determined and generally adopted, the expected productivity gains must be negotiated and made known within each establishment. This will lead establishments to adopt a quality approach and to streamline management. This long and necessarily complex approach is in some respects revolutionary by comparison with current practices; but it will have no tangible impact unless the productivity gains are then distributed. This final condition must be fulfilled; it is all the more necessary in education systems that are dominated by state monopoly. If individual teachers, teacher teams or those establishments that generate rises in productivity do not share, at least in part, in the gains, either by salary improvement or by investment in learning materials, multimedia, etc., they will lack an incentive to embrace the new approach. Quite the opposite. No successful company would ever dream of introducing increased productivity arrangements without first involving staff in negotiations on dividing up the gains. The educational world does not always involve its staff to the same extent. Productivity levels can be more profitably discussed when management is sufficiently flexible so as to allow the individuals or teams to share in the productivity gains which they, after all, are generating. [1]

## Upgrading the job of teacher/trainer and heads of establishments

183. Progress along the lines described above would give society more confidence in its schools — where that confidence has been lost — and thus all those associated with them. However, specific measures should be targeted not only at teachers but also headteachers.

---

[1] In Sweden, a new remuneration system for all teaching staff has actively improved quality and furthered school development. The basic idea is that teachers must actively contribute to the development of the schools in which they work. Those involved in determining salary levels have agreed that this be considered an important criterion for establishing the remuneration of individual teachers.

184.   **Teachers** play a primordial role because they are the only people in our societies providing a service of such a marked multidimensional character. Contemporary trends are that their role is becoming even more multi-faceted, because it increasingly incorporates social, behavioural, civic, economic and technological dimensions.

Teaching is an activity that can less and less be viewed from within a subject disciplinary logic, but many teachers do not have the training or experience to cope with this greatly extended role. While teachers have to face up to new challenges posed by changed social and economic conditions, it is clear that they should benefit from high quality pre-service teacher education, supported by induction processes in their early period as teachers and be sustained throughout their careers by varied forms of in-service training and professional development.

Therefore, the Study Group considers great emphasis should be placed on teacher education and training. Furthermore, the conditions of work of teachers and the equipment provided must be of a character which gives them a reasonable opportunity of achieving high level performance in the classroom. If they are to liaise more successfully and more openly with parents and the community, this must be acknowledged and supported. Where the teachers are located in contexts of great deprivation and socio-economic disadvantage, a supportive, intersectoral range of professional services needs to be available with which such teachers can co-operate for the benefit of their pupils.

185.   The question of the in-service education and training is particularly urgent in that the age-profile of serving teachers is now quite top-heavy, or at least imbalanced, in a number of countries. This can be looked at from a number of very different angles. The need for in-service education and training for teachers is evident and, without doubt, the profession could see a strong development of self-directed continuing training. Member States have opted for various solutions here. In some countries, teachers' working hours are expressed in terms of contact hours (except for upper secondary vocational education); individual teachers pursue their own professional development and follow the progress of their pupils in non-contact-time (France, Belgium, Germany, Ireland, Luxembourg). In other countries the employment contract distinguishes, on an annual basis, contact and non-contact working hours; in some cases — for example, Finland and Sweden — in-service education and training time is an explicit part of working hours. Another approach is to establish

in-service education and training provision for teachers, and make them more or less compulsory. [1]

186. Teachers' in-service training needs are varied and therefore demand flexible and varied responses by providers. In-service provision covers a wide range of aspects of the job of teaching, from updating subject-specific knowledge through acquiring new methodological skills and tools (including IT) to school development and ways of building links with family or community links — to mention but a few. Courses are offered under varied kinds of schedules (from one-off evening seminars to higher degree courses), in a range of locations and institutions (from within the school itself to distance universities), and by different groups of personnel (from colleagues themselves to academic experts). In some countries, there is an established tradition of in-service training that works directly in schools and with teachers themselves. Key criteria for success in teacher in-service education and training include good needs assessment, appropriate course design, active commitment from participants, the availability of high quality training personnel, and continuous course evaluation processes.

A further issue is generating in teachers a full appreciation of the demands placed on their students by employment in the modern world. The main effective way of doing this is to get teachers repeated spells of work experience and job shadowing in industry and commerce.

187. As for trainers, the problem is completely different, because most of the time the market decides. The Study Group takes the view that this should remain so. Although there is a need for better information about this particular market to make it more transparent and to ensure that appropriate standards prevail, it would be a grave mistake to contemplate introducing various kinds of special status based on paper qualifications. This is a corporatist approach that is spreading quickly throughout all sectors, and works to the advantage of those who are already in the occupation. In this sense, to upgrade the training profession disadvantages prospective new entrants, whose access chances will be made more difficult. By contrast, one way of improving the quality of vocational training is to provide in-service education and training courses for trainers and to assess what they have actually learned. Such courses do not necessarily have to be provided within higher education establishments.

---

[1] Cf. Eurydice, 'In-service teacher training in the European Union and in the EFTA/EEA countries' 1995.

188. Generally speaking, heads' powers ought to be reinforced and in-service education and training should also be provided for them. The aim is that each establishment operates as an innovative body with its own goals and is capable of mobilising the means necessary to achieve them. This presupposes that schools are able to organise themselves to better effect as teaching teams (thus having a major say in the choice of their staff); are able to pay incentives to the best teachers out of their own funds; and become learning organisations. A school needs to have a collective memory, a culture, and to develop a knowledge base that comes from accumulated pedagogic experience. Heads should also experience other working cultures. Therefore, it is highly desirable for innovative companies to play some kind of role in the training of heads.

Heads of educational establishments carry the responsibility of assuring the establishment's mission — a genuine and explicit educational mission, which does not often exist. The mission must include aims, means to attain these aims, an implementation strategy and the evaluation of outcomes in relation to aims. The mission-in-action necessitates working in groups and teams, and involves all the players (pupils, teachers, ancillary staff and the head), who are called upon to establish between themselves a community solidarity.

Schools that succeed in their mission are also those that bring external players, in particular parents, into the process of mission design and implementation. All European educational systems have implicitly or explicitly recognised the positive contribution parents' participation makes to school life, and have translated this recognition into ways of involving them in the functioning of educational establishments themselves. Since the 1970s, in Denmark, parents form the majority membership of basic school management bodies; other countries, such as Spain or Greece, only began to move in similar directions from the mid-1980s; Sweden did so recently, too. The primary and secondary educational reforms that have taken place over the last ten years all reinforce parents' roles in relation to schools. However, one can observe that parents' roles are most typically limited to consultation in the context of school administration and management, whereas they are most commonly excluded from pedagogic activity.[1]

---

[1] Cf. Eurydice, 'The role of parents in educational systems' 1996.

# Undertaking evaluation on a broad scale

189. It follows from the above that education systems will not evolve without the active participation of the basic players involved. Their everyday practice in their own establishments will change the way our systems operate. Therefore, these players must be given the appropriate means to exercise their autonomy and to find a sound balance between inducements (or pressures) and support at establishment level. Initially, then, evaluation is indispensable because it generates the information that provides — through the 'mirror effect' — a basis for continually re-evaluating one's own position.

190. However, evaluation also has a second and equally important function. Publicly accessible, comprehensible and well-founded evaluation provides a clear picture of the types of education and training available. This greater transparency is necessary so that users know what they are doing when they choose a particular field, establishment or training course. Thus, sound evaluation will greatly improve the average productivity of the education and training systems, since the learner can exercise free choice.

191. Evaluation must aim for comparisons over space and time of education and training outcomes. Therefore, precise definition of what is to be evaluated, and the criteria by which this is to be evaluated, is essential. In particular, evaluation should focus on learning outcomes: what have pupils learned? However, evaluation must also take account of the effects of environmental context; evaluation should neither inhibit nor punish.

192. Therefore, the Study Group recommends focusing on the concept of 'added value' as one of the main possible guidelines for evaluation procedures. In an educational context, added value is the difference between the knowledge and skills learners possess when they enter an establishment or course, and what they possess when they leave or finish. Some Member States have set up evaluation procedures along these lines, and expanding this approach across the European Union would provide a basis for comparison. This concept of relativity is important, notably to allow (i) teachers to alter their approaches, and (ii) the authorities to measure the return on public spending more easily. Of course, this does not obviate the need to evaluate what has been gained in absolute terms. This gives learners the information they need to select a particular educational establishment or training centre. Users themselves are less interested in a school's added value performance; they

134

are interested in absolute learning outcomes and their recognition and exchange value on the labour market. The value-added concept is also useful when it comes to evaluating the effectiveness of multimedia IT approaches. There can always be a risk that this will be technology-driven rather than education-driven. This risk can be avoided by locating the evaluation parameters clearly in educational value-added terms together with cost effectiveness.

## Making education and training more open to all forms of co-operation

193. Our education and training systems — in particular our education systems — must develop a wide range of partnerships with the other players in society. This point has been made in connection with education-industry relations. Vocational training will not develop satisfactorily without a firm partnership with companies. The same is true for social cohesion, where partnerships with local authorities and the voluntary sector are crucial.

194. But this move to more openness should also involve the players themselves, first and foremost teachers, who need to be able to continue to pursue their civic mission and to participate actively in creating the learning society. In particular, this implies teacher involvement in the development and application of information technologies and of lifelong learning. Teachers who are fully conscious of their crucial civic mission in life could contribute to all forms of lifelong learning, not only within their usual setting, but also as a pivot between informal knowledge exchange networks which might cover specific geographic regions or might concentrate on specific groups. Making progress towards the learning society will benefit education systems and teachers, provided they play their part in bringing it about.

195. Partnerships maintained by individual establishments or teachers themselves must be based on balanced relations between the partners. When schools form partnerships with companies or industrial sectors, they do not wish to be viewed simply as service providers. Companies that provide training, work experience placements and apprenticeship contracts are in the same position: they must have a say in the curriculum and its validation. Some difficulties are already emerging in connection with the introduction of lifelong learning. Where public funds are used to develop this concept, a market immediately appears, accompanied by power plays. This is already happening in some cases, hidden beneath

questions of principle. Existing educational providers will prefer to see lifelong learning focused on target groups, because this offers an opportunity to institutionalise their activity in the long term. By contrast, the business sector and enterprises themselves will prefer a more open system, like a supermarket of educational products widely available to individuals.

196. Therefore, efforts must be undertaken at European level to set up legal structures permitting the development of such partnerships, which should involve all the social partners. It is difficult to envisage balanced partnerships between schools and other players based on current legal instruments, especially in Member States where educational provision is essentially governed by the State and public authorities.

197. In the course of its discussions on economic activity and the Information Society, but also on citizenship and social cohesion, the Study Group is very much interested in the developments in continuing training and, more generally, in lifelong learning.

With reference to the debates on competitivity and employment, it appears important to promote a strategy of continually raising competence levels. Apart from the efforts made to renew and significantly to adapt education and initial training systems, this strategy necessitates a strengthened mobilisation of continuing training and a clear orientation towards its development on a large scale, in the interest of responding well to contemporary changes.

Opting for this scenario is vital for Europe. In a labour market which continues to be characterised by relatively low levels of mobility and by bottlenecks at initial entry to employment, the development of continuing training appears — at least in the short term — as the best way of enhancing employee skills; it is employees who are the first to experience the socio-organisational changes taking place in enterprises. The objective of continuously promoting the enhancement of skills must become central to the policies pursued by the different players involved and to company-internal and labour market management mechanisms.

As far as public employment policies are concerned, similar preoccupations seem to be developing in favour of active employment policies in which access to, and the promotion of competencies are playing a greater part. Training measures have significantly developed at the same time as has the struggle to reduce unemployment together with increasingly frequent questioning of the real effectiveness of expenditures and their contribution to an active policy to get the jobless back into paid employment.

Continuing training provision has mainly developed within a market logic and the development of a service activity directed towards companies. In this context, three questions appear to emerge: the trends in costs, the quality of provision, and the evaluation of outcomes. The development of continuing training and its establishment as a recognised economic sector implies that, for the three points noted, important progress has been made and rendered transparent for users.

Without having been able totally to assess their consequences, the Study Group's discussions have equally underlined the new opportunities offered both by the development of the tools of the Information Society within enterprises and by new approaches towards the division of time.

On the first point, some companies are clearly pushing the spread of 'learning situations' as good ways of enhancing skills rather than as formal training. Continuously promoting the enhancement of skills thus blends in with changes in work organisation, work contents and hierarchical relations. In this sense, the aim of promoting individual and collective competencies amongst employees is becoming a priority management objective.

The issue of the organisation, division and use of time is rendered more uncertain in the light of question-marks over whether or not working hours will be significantly reduced. However, there is some evidence in company policy and in agreements between social partners of renewed interest in linking the reorganisation/reduction of working hours and the development of 'training time'. Without doubt, a 'reservoir' of flexibility and of resources exists here, one which deserves to be more fully explored.

## What action should the European Union pursue?

198. Article 126 of the Treaty limits the European Union's avenues of action as regards the organisation and operation of education and training systems, which clearly fall within national competence. The Study Group takes the view that this is an advantage, given the desirability of having a number of pathways to achieving similar ends. On the other hand, no interpretation of the concept of subsidiarity should be so restrictive that it prevents Europe — following discussion among the Member States and in collaboration with them — from declaring what the main common aims

of our education and training systems are to be. Europe must also contribute, through initiatives and projects, to the wide dissemination of best practice and must encourage progress towards those aims. The Study Group takes the view that these efforts require more close collaboration with the Member States than has been the case to date. If we wish to lend concrete expression to the European vision that we offer to our young people and to develop lifelong learning, then education and training must be accorded a more central position in European preoccupations.

199. With this in mind, the guidelines for Union action on education and training systems could be to:

- proclaim a general European aim that serves as a guide for the different systems: such as the one proposed in this report: 'make it possible to give everyone the opportunity for personal development and to achieve at the high levels required by the new international environment and to acquire the resources needed for social integration'. The declared aim should make it clear that Europe (i) wishes to remain competitive, but (ii) will not resign itself to having an irreducible core of socially excluded persons; and (iii) wants to promote the development of the person and the education of active citizens;

- anchoring this goal either in the Treaty or in another legal foundation;

- secure the financial means to achieve this goal: if we wish to see Europe placed amongst the best educational standards in the world (Japan, Finland, USA), it will be necessary to devote a full percentage point of GDP resources in addition to that spent today.

It would also be necessary to:

- develop initial and continuing teacher education and training by the identification and discovery of best practice;

- institute a specific programme of exchanges and in-service education and training for headteachers and directors of education and training establishments;

- encourage innovative learning practices in educational establishments and training centres;

- pinpoint, study and disseminate good practice with respect to productivity and the search for quality in educational establishments and training centres;

- devise common methods for the evaluation of education and training based on experiences in national levels, in order to benefit from a comparative dimension;

- study the possibility of a legal and operational framework at European level that facilitates the development of partnerships between schools, companies and local authorities;

- look into the possibility of setting up venture capital companies to encourage the development of innovative teaching and learning products.

# Statistical annex

200.	Recent OECD studies on human resources investment indicators and on the funding of lifelong learning for everyone, and European Commission studies on employment in Europe, raise questions as to the extent of investment on education and training made by the Member States of the European Union and in certain cases prompt comparison with what is done in the USA and Japan. However, due caution must be taken when making comparisons because certain results are difficult to compare, for definitions may differ from country to country, as can the areas covered and the reference periods. The figures quoted are often no more than estimates and give only an approximate idea. The figures on the direct and indirect costs of education and training methods are incomplete, making it very difficult to assess results and the cost effectiveness of investment in education and training. The data available on continuing training are not standardised in Europe and there is no one definition of 'training' which is valid across the different countries. In addition, there is a particular shortage of information on business sector training expenditure. It is nonetheless important to progress on this front, for all political decision-makers have to face up to problems of resources and simply must have information on the cost effectiveness of any investment for which they opt.

201.	The principle of access to lifelong training is accepted in all Member States and initially appears to be the subject of consensus requiring resources and institutional reform which most Member States are not prepared to countenance. While paying lip service to the idea, Member States generally continue to place the emphasis on initial training and are not necessarily prepared to modify structures which are not conducive to lifelong learning.

202. Expenditure, particularly total public expenditure, for all levels of teaching (pre-school, primary, secondary and higher) for public and private establishments are constantly increasing in all EU countries as they are in the USA and Japan. Between 1985 and 1992 they rose in Spain for example from MECU 8 882 to MECU 17 731.

203. Expenditure on education as a percentage of GDP in 1992 is also known, for all levels of teaching and by type of establishment (public and private, subsidized or not). [1] There are significant differences from one country to another in the portion of GDP earmarked for public establishments, with the Nordic countries (Finland, Sweden and Denmark) spending the greatest share (over 6%), most of the other countries allocating 4-5% of their GDP, with the exception of the Netherlands which spends only 1.7% of its GDP on public establishments. However, these differences disappear if account is taken of expenditure on public and private establishments considered together. The American rate is similar to that of the Nordic countries, while the Japanese rate is the same as that of the other European countries.

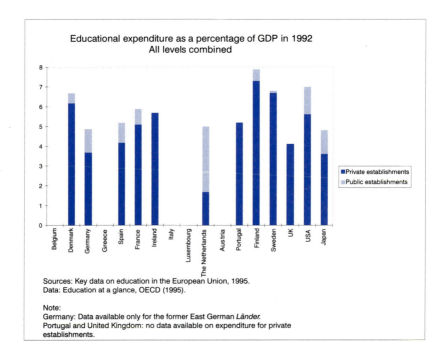

Educational expenditure as a percentage of GDP in 1992
All levels combined

Private establishments
Public establishments

Sources: Key data on education in the European Union, 1995.
Data: Education at a glance, OECD (1995).

Note:
Germany: Data available only for the former East German *Länder*.
Portugal and United Kingdom: no data available on expenditure for private establishments.

---

[1] 'Education at a glance', OECD indicators 1995, Educational expenditure as a percentage of GDP in 1992, all levels combined, Annex 13.

204. A look at expenditure on education as a percentage of GDP for primary and secondary education shows that in the case of public establishments, it is once again the Nordic countries which spend the greatest share of their GDP on primary and secondary education (over 4%) along with the UK, Portugal and the USA.[1]

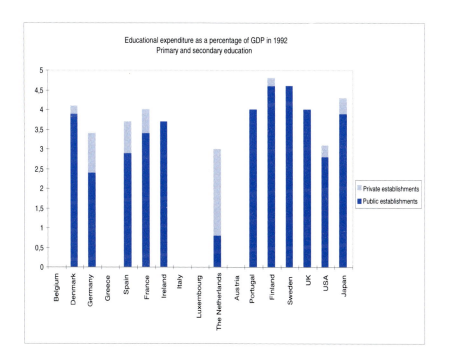

Educational expenditure as a percentage of GDP in 1992
Primary and secondary education

205. In the case of higher education (not considering research), and including all types of establishments, the Member States spend between 0.9% and 1% of their GDP, with the exception of the UK and Japan which devote only 0.8%, whereas Denmark, Ireland, the Netherlands and Finland allocate over 1.3% and the USA 2.5%. The significant portion of GDP spent on private establishments should be noted in the case of the UK and in Japan where it even exceeds the proportion earmarked for public establishments, and also in the Netherlands and the USA.[2]

---

[1] 'Education at a glance', OECD indicators 1995, Educational expenditure as a percentage of GDP in 1992, primary and secondary education, Annex 14.

[2] 'Education at a glance', OECD indicators 1995, Educational expenditure as a percentage of GDP in 1992, higher education, Annex 15.

143

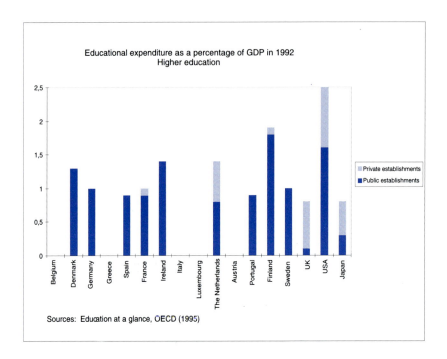

Educational expenditure as a percentage of GDP in 1992
Higher education

Legend: Private establishments / Public establishments

Sources: Education at a glance, OECD (1995)

206. After looking at the percentage of GDP spent by type of teaching, it is interesting to study for each country the expenditure per pupil by level of teaching in 1992 in absolute terms (expressed in ECU).[1] It has to be borne in mind, when interpreting figures for early childhood education, that the Nordic countries often provide day and evening nurseries the cost of which is included in *per capita* expenditure, which explains why in Finland, Sweden and Denmark, expenditure is around ECU 5 000 whereas in all the other countries, the USA and Japan included, the expenditure per pupils is ECU 1 300 to ECU 2 700.

Five European countries (the Nordic countries of Finland, Sweden and Denmark plus Austria and Italy) spend over ECU 3 000 per primary school pupil; expenditure is particularly high in the USA (ECU 4 445). It is low in Ireland (ECU 1 405) and in Spain (ECU 1 802).

Moving on to the secondary level, four countries spend over ECU 4 800; these are Sweden, Austria and Belgium along with the USA. They are

[1] 'Education at a glance', OECD indicators 1995, expenditure per pupil of early childhood education 1992, Expenditure per pupil of primary education 1992, Expenditure per student in secondary education 1992, and Expenditure per student in higher education 1992, Annex 16.

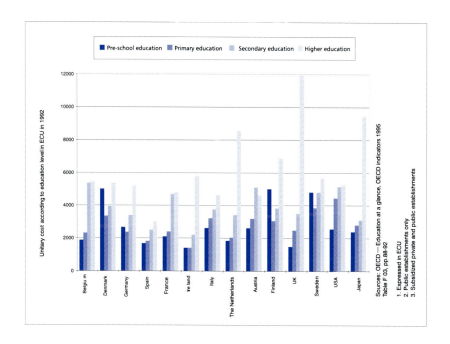

Sources: OECD — Education at a glance, OECD Indicators 1995
Table F 03, pp.88-92

1. Expressed in ECU
2. Public establishments only
3. Subsidized private and public establishments

followed closely by France, with ECU 4 460, while Ireland and Spain are well behind (ECU 2 195 and ECU 2 494 respectively).

Things vary much more - by a ratio of 1 to 3 - when it comes to *per capita* expenditure in higher education. Three countries are above the ECU 8 500 mark; these are the UK (ECU 11 952), the Netherlands (ECU 8 550) and Japan (ECU 9 407). The same applies to the USA where the cost of a student in the public sector is ECU 5 240, compared with over ECU 15 000 in the private sector. The other European countries, with the exception of Spain, Austria and Italy, spend in the region of ECU 4 7000.

Predictably enough, the richer countries generally spend more per pupil/student than the poorer countries, but there is no systematic pattern and there are substantial differences between the countries.

207. These indicators give some idea of the public and private contributions to the organisation of education and training, mainly as regards the sources of public funding. But little information is to hand on continuing training that targets the over-25s. 'Continuing training' means all systematic and organised activities open to people seeking to obtain fresh qualifications

in their current jobs or with a view to a future job, to increase their income potential or, more generally, to improve their promotion prospects. The European Commission has conducted a labour force survey which takes account of people in training during the four weeks immediately prior to the survey. The percentage of persons in employment aged 25 and over is low and would appear to be consistently under 6% for men and women alike, except in the Netherlands, Denmark and the UK. A new survey is currently being conducted but no results are yet to hand.

208. In order to have the basis for an estimate of what lifelong learning for everyone would cost, outside the school system, the OECD figures make it possible to calculate for each EC country the adults aged 25-64 educated up to first secondary level in 1992; the resulting figure is high: over 46 million adults.[1] If these figures are multiplied by training cost estimates from other sources, total costs would, depending on the scenario envisaged, be around 2-4% of GDP.

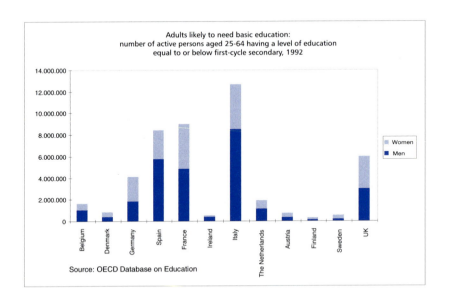

Source: OECD Database on Education

---

[1] OECD database on education, 'Adults likely to need basic education: number of active persons aged 25-64 having a level of education of up to the first secondary level', 1992, Annex 17.

209. The OECD endeavours to gauge the impact of education on training leading to a qualification by using as an indicator, not figures on 'human resources', but data on the level of educational attainment of the adult population. The levels of education are defined in accordance with the International Standard Classification of Education (ISCED) as applicable to educational programmes in the various countries. The distribution of the adult population as a function of the highest level of education reached reveals wide divergencies from country to country whereas expenditure on education as a percentage of GDP highlights other divergencies affecting the same countries.[1] The OECD has also calculated the average number of years of schooling for the adult population on the basis of studies completed and an average estimate of the cumulative duration of studies which led to this level of education.[2]

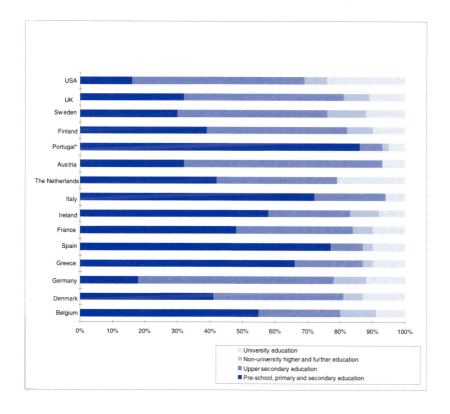

[1] 'Education at a glance', OECD indicators 1995, Educational attainment of the population, Annex 18.

[2] 'Indicators for investment in human resources: feasibility study', 1996, average number of years of study in the adult population in 1992, Annex 19.

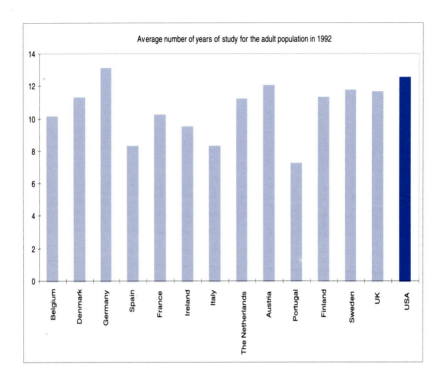

Average number of years of study for the adult population in 1992

210. These indicators do not take account of the contribution of education to the acquisition of skills and qualifications. This can be done by using the findings of international surveys of school results, particularly those of the International Association for the Evaluation of Educational Achievement (IEA), but the results of the surveys give only some measure (as regards reading, mathematics, the sciences) of the impact of education on the 9-14 age groups in the countries covered by the IEA surveys. Nevertheless, it is worthwhile comparing the school results with the figures for the human resources stock in the adult population.

211. The OECD and the European Commission have also endeavoured to evaluate the impact of education and training on people's occupational situation. The average annual earnings of the 25-64 age group can thus be compared by level of education and sex.[1] It emerges clearly that the average annual earnings are systematically related to

---

[1] 'Education at a glance', OECD indicators 1995, Education and earnings, Annex 20.

148

the level of education. The same applies, but the other way round, when a comparison is made of the rate of unemployment broken down by level of education of men and women over the different countries. [1]

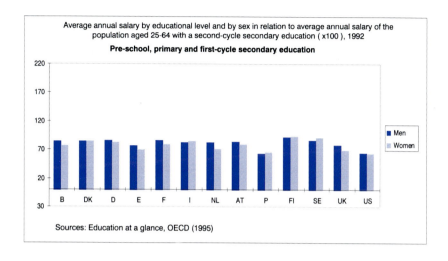

Average annual salary by educational level and by sex in relation to average annual salary of the population aged 25-64 with a second-cycle secondary education ( x100 ), 1992

**Pre-school, primary and first-cycle secondary education**

Sources: Education at a glance, OECD (1995)

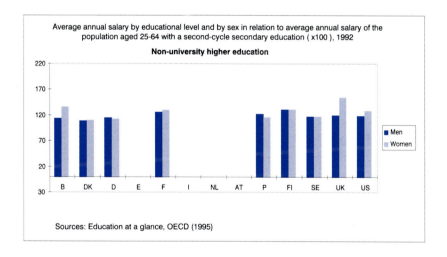

Average annual salary by educational level and by sex in relation to average annual salary of the population aged 25-64 with a second-cycle secondary education ( x100 ), 1992

**Non-university higher education**

Sources: Education at a glance, OECD (1995)

---

[1] 'Employment in Europe', Commission of the European Communities 1995, Unemployment rates of men aged 25-59 by education level, 1994, Annex 21.

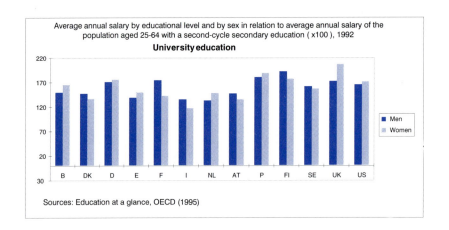

Average annual salary by educational level and by sex in relation to average annual salary of the population aged 25-64 with a second-cycle secondary education ( x100 ), 1992

**University education**

Sources: Education at a glance, OECD (1995)

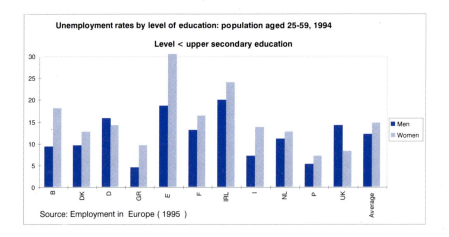

**Unemployment rates by level of education: population aged 25-59, 1994**

**Level < upper secondary education**

Source: Employment in Europe ( 1995 )

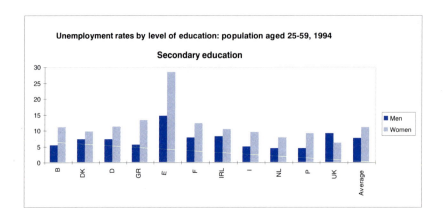

**Unemployment rates by level of education: population aged 25-59, 1994**

**Secondary education**

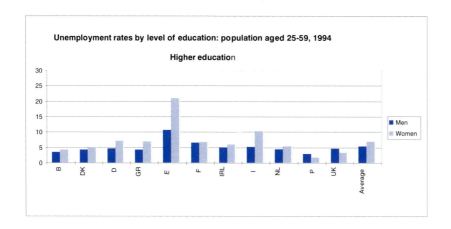

**Unemployment rates by level of education: population aged 25-59, 1994**

**Higher education**

212. Be it initial training or continuing training, it is clear that the effort needed in all countries carries a heavy cost. How should the financial burden be appropriately broken down over the public/state sector, the local authorities, families and the people concerned themselves? This is the question put in a recent OECD Education Committee (December 1995) which examined how to fund lifelong learning. No significant figures are as yet available. An OECD survey is currently being undertaken on this.

213. The funding of lifelong learning beyond compulsory schooling raises particularly tricky problems. While the employment policies conducted in the Community countries imply substantial public sector aid for training to offset the initial training gaps of unemployed persons, the training provided by companies or linked to employment is generally paid for by employers and sometimes by the employees. In-company training financed by the public sector is exceptional.

214. Although some people opt for lifelong learning just out of pleasure, as part of their leisure activities, or with no employment-related ends in mind, continuing training is generally an employment-related investment made at a given time and designed to bear fruit later. As stressed in the OECD Education Committee report (December 1995, the payer-beneficiary tandem is a lop-sided arrangement in which investment in lifelong training generates immediate cost whereas the advantages take some time to filter through. In terms of investment input this could prove a disincentive, particularly to individuals, but also to the public authorities and employers. More reliable data than those available to day are needed on:

- the cost for any country of not investing in lifelong training;

- evaluating all-round training requirements;

- the cost-effectiveness of different continuing training arrangements, with the emphasis on containing costs more efficiently.

Like the OECD, the Study Group feels this would put us in a better position to assess the instances in which high social returns would justify greater input from the public authorities and those instances in which high individual returns would justify greater input on the part of the persons concerned.

# Annex on the comparison of education and training systems

215. Beyond the various monographs and comparisons of education and training systems which already exist, the Study Group is in favour of the proposal for a programme of studies with a view to comparative analysis of systems based on selected horizontal themes likely to throw light on the working arrangements of systems and how to influence trends therein. These horizontal themes are:

   a) homogeneity of provision: principle of the 'common school', diversification of syllabi in basic general education, a common foundation;

   b) arrangements for access to higher education: selection, grants, elitist or open systems, links with research;

   c) autonomy of establishments: decentralisation of decision-making, autonomy in managing resources, recruitment requirements for teachers, teaching methods;

   d) involvement of the economic players: educational partnerships for on- and off-the-job training, secondment of higher education academic staff as schoolteachers, definition of syllabi;

   e) evaluation systems: level and arrangements for evaluating costs and results, impact on allocation of resources, publicising performance figures.

European Commission

**Study group on education and training — Report — Accomplishing Europe through education and training**

Luxembourg: Office for Official Publications of the European Communities

1997 — 152 pp. — 17.6 x 25 cm

ISBN 92-827-9493-8